RISE

RISE

HOW EMPOWERING WOMEN
ELEVATES US ALL

SHANA ABRAHAM

NEW DEGREE PRESS

RISE

How Empowering Women Elevates Us All

ISBN   978-1-64137-984-7   *Paperback*
          978-1-64137-875-8   *Kindle Ebook*
          978-1-64137-876-5   *Ebook*

DEFINING COLOR TERMINOLOGY IN RISE

Color terminology has dominated racial discourse across the world for centuries. Because we commonly use the color-based racial designations "Black" and "White," color is often misused as a synonym for race. But there is no "Brown" race, and even the U.S. Supreme Court hasn't conclusively defined what it means to be Brown in America.

The designation "brown" is applied differently throughout the world. The term may be applied to those of South Asian descent, who often identify as "Brown people," but also to Latinx populations, Indigenous peoples, Native Hawaiian, Pacific Islanders, African, and African-American populations, and to those of to those of Arab and Middle Eastern descent.

For the purposes of this book, the term "Brown" is used to refer to color, to one's visible appearance, and not as a synonym for race. The terms "Brown girl," and "Brown women" are applied broadly to include many girls and women of color who do not self-identify as Black or White. When I describe myself as a "brown girl" or "brown woman," it is a reference to my South Asian (specifically Indian) heritage and cultural identity.

Admittedly, the social construct is imperfect. To collapse diverse peoples into an ethnic monolith is to imply that they share a single identity when, in fact, they do not. The fact is that the struggles, ideas, histories, and experiences of any people cannot be teased apart into color-based or racial designations. The challenges and disparities that every population faces are different and nuanced, and it is important to recognize that while there are overall trends to be acknowledged, each group of people have a variety of lived experiences that should be respected.

Please use the sources in the appendix to clarify the exact populations referenced in the study, should you wish to know who the findings of such studies were specifically attributed to.

To the women who raised me, shaped me,
and continue to stand by my side:

You are my heart.

CONTENTS

———

INTRODUCTION

———

You walk onto the bus at the end of the day and shrug your bookbag onto the seat next to you, tuning out the chattering schoolgirls around you. It was a long day of hard work, but you are satisfied. While it wasn't easy to attain, your education will help you create change. You think about the countless girls denied education in your community, but you remain hopeful your studies will help you advocate for them in the near future. Suddenly, you're snapped back into reality as a masked gunman steps onto the bus, demanding to know which one of these girls is the one called "Yousafzai." As all the girls automatically dart their eyes toward you, you can't imagine how your life will change from that moment as the man aims his gun at your head.

You probably recognize this as the story of Malala Yousafzai, the young woman who survived being shot in the head by the Taliban. Today, Malala is one of the most prominent advocates of education, especially for girls. Not only is she the youngest person to ever receive the Nobel Peace Prize but she has stayed true to her roots and become a role model for women everywhere as she humbly advocates for those in need.

I have always been inspired by her. Just by being herself, she combats the stereotype that female activists are always "loud and angry." In fact, she is the very opposite: calm, collected, and always looking to spread her message peacefully. Malala is the epitome of what it means to be a young female changemaker.

But what is a changemaker? The term was first popularized by former United States President Bill Clinton when describing his wife Hillary at the 2016 Democratic National Convention as the "best darn changemaker [he'd] ever seen."[1] It was then adopted by the Ashoka organization, which defined it as "one who desires change in the world and, by gathering knowledge and resources, makes that change happen."[2] According to Ashoka, changemakers are tenacious about the greater good, personally connected to the issues they want to solve, and lean on a supportive network to accomplish their goals.[3]

Malala's story seems almost like the plot of a movie; the fact that it happened in real life paradoxically makes it seem even more fantastical. When we think of the women creating change in the world, we immediately think of these dramatic stories. After all, being shot at point-blank range and surviving is nothing short of miraculous.

---

1   Jacob Pramuk, "Bill Clinton: Hillary Is 'The Best Darn Change Maker I've Ever Known,'" CNBC, updated July 27, 2016.

2   Benjamin Hendricks, "What Is a Changemaker?", Observations of a Changemaker, accessed June 8, 2020.

3   Reem Rahman, Kris Herbst, and Tim Scheu, "What Is a Changemaker?" Fast Company, August 4, 2016.

Yet most people don't have these types of life-altering experiences, so where does that leave the rest of us? Can anyone be a changemaker?

As I've researched the topic of female empowerment, I've come to realize a simple truth. With time, discipline, and the right resources, any woman can make a change. Regardless of her age, education level, life experiences, or position in society, one woman can inspire and impact millions of lives.

Truly, one woman is enough. There are many ways to create an impact, and through this book, I hope to make more women realize each of us can be our own Malala—and follow in the footsteps of the millions of others like her.

Women make up half the world's population, but they often lack recognition for the value they bring to our society, rarely receiving the full rights they deserve. According to the United Nations, 750 million women and girls were married before the age of eighteen.[4] At least two hundred million women across thirty countries have undergone female genital mutilation.[5] One in five women and girls have experienced physical and/or sexual violence by an intimate partner within the last twelve months, yet forty-nine countries don't have laws to protect women from such violence.[6]

---

4   "Goal 5: Achieve Gender Equality and Empower All Women and Girls," United Nations Sustainable Development Goals, United Nations, accessed June 8, 2020.

5   Ibid.

6   Ibid.

Only 13 percent of the world's agricultural landholders are women, even though roughly two billion people derive their livelihood from agriculture.[7] No matter where one looks, women are consistently hindered from achieving a higher quality of life. Whether it be opportunities for economic development, the chance to be educated, the freedom to enter into marriage willingly, or personal safety, the list of necessary freedoms denied to women is endless.

This is not to say the world has not made great strides in empowering females. We've made progress in many different sectors in the past few decades. More than one hundred countries have allocated part of their budgets for efforts toward gender equality. In forty-six countries, women now hold more than 30 percent of seats in national parliament in at least one chamber. In Southern Asia, a girl's risk of childhood marriage has dropped by over 40 percent since 2000.[8]

While these are all wonderful achievements, they're still *not enough*. One hundred countries may have allocated part of their budgets toward gender equality, but this leaves dozens of countries having yet to make such an allocation. After all, 23.7 percent female representation in national parliaments is still far from parity.[9] The risk of childhood marriage has dropped for many girls across the world, but it has not been completely eradicated. Millions of girls are still at risk!

---

7   Ibid, FAO, *World Food and Agriculture Statistical Pocketbook 2018*, United Nations.

8   "Goal 5: Achieve Gender Equality and Empower All Women and Girls," United Nations.

9   Ibid.

When you look at the world and all its problems, it's easy to become overwhelmed and believe there's no helping our global situation. It seems that for every solution we create, a new problem arises in its place.

But humanity has always had an affinity for creating change and for improving society. As time goes on, we see more young people step into the limelight as leaders of such change: people like Malala Yousafzai, Greta Thunberg, Nadya Okamoto, Deja Foxx, and Angeline Makore. Many young people, specifically young *women*, have chosen to fight for what they believe in.

While people of all generations can advocate for change, there is a special power in having young people step up to create the change for which their senior counterparts cannot or will not advocate. There are over 1.8 billion young people between the ages of ten and twenty-four in the world, with 90 percent of them in developing countries.[10] While they are often considered the most unwise and inexperienced members of society, young people have great power. I believe a different sense of responsibility, connection, and motivation exists when we are called to action by our peers. If we can mobilize even a small percentage of these young people, there is no limit to the positive impact that will follow their efforts.

It's easy to believe the narrative that certain people are just "born" to change the world. It seems like success was written

---

10   UNFPA, "Adolescent and Youth Demographics: A Brief Overview," United Nations Population Fund, accessed June 8, 2020.

in their destinies. But I know a lot more than destiny is at play when it comes to these women creating immense impact.

As I began studying global health in college, I became interested in female empowerment. Even though I've listened to countless lectures on the dire situations of millions of women who live in horrible, unimaginable conditions, I have also learned about the millions of survivors.

I wanted to learn more about the women who made a difference in themselves, their communities, and even the world. I've realized the power in having a voice and using it to drive impact. The field of global health is constantly producing research showing women are at the center of many interventions, due to their ability to influence the health of the communities they live in.

All communities benefit from the empowerment of women through gaining health education, financial freedom, and/ or human rights. I've looked at countless studies and heard dozens of global leaders speak to the benefits of prioritizing women—trillions of dollars in our global economy could be recovered, community health would further improve, and more children would be in school.[11] Once I learned about all these benefits, I started to wonder how I could spread the importance of female empowerment to more people, especially as I recognized how this has played out in my own life.

---

11   Sarah Emerson, "Empowered Women Are Key to Transforming Communities," Project Concern International, March 9, 2016.

My parents immigrated from India—a country well-known for its patriarchal history. It constantly felt like the patriarchy was breathing down my neck, especially when I had to fight to leave the house after it got dark or when family members constantly reminded me of the importance of marriage. However, my life was a lot more aligned with feminism than I realized.

My mother has been the breadwinner of our family for as long as I can remember. I watched her work tirelessly to keep our household running and her family happy. My parents grew up in a culture where women were responsible for all the "domestic" tasks, so my father was not inclined to share the domestic workload equally. My mom's share of housework should've merited an additional salary on top of her professional career. But when my sisters and I pointed out this imbalance, my mom would grumble for a bit and then reply with something like, "Who else will take care of the household and do all these chores if I don't?"

To this day, when I state my desire to maintain an equal balance with my future partner regarding domestic work, my mom often laughs and sarcastically replies, "Good luck finding a man that's willing to do that." I usually aggressively roll my eyes in response, but in my head, it's difficult to process that she still believes this.

Knowing this can't be universally true, I often silently fume at how much our conversation frustrates me. It's easy to see my mom is referencing centuries of gender norms that have dictated the roles our society seeks to fulfill. Yet even though I grew up understanding this gender bias, specifically how

South Asian culture continues to struggle with changing these perceptions, I successfully changed my perspective because I grew up trying to balance two cultures with differing viewpoints.

Being raised in the United States gave me new ideas for how my future could look, emphasizing the American values of freedom and choice—the ideas that encouraged us to create our own destiny rather than stick to old traditions. My parents have their reservations about what their daughters adopted from American culture, such as our incessant desire for autonomy in every aspect of our life and lack of inhibition when debating with them.

However, they ultimately immigrated to America to provide their children a chance for a better life. This goal is inherently connected to America's better academic opportunities, and, therefore, my parents have always encouraged my sisters and me to study and reach our highest potential. As a result, I grew up believing this was the norm for most girls. After all, didn't most parents want what was best for their kids? Yet as the years passed, I realized not everyone had the opportunities I was fortunate enough to have. But even with these opportunities, life continued to provide obstacles to my success.

As I continued learning about social change, my determination grew to create widespread impact. But I was constantly told to "be realistic." Many of the people I'd assumed would unconditionally support me instead labeled my dreams as too "far-fetched." They constantly reminded me creating my own path would be difficult and encouraged me to pick a more conventional route.

But I didn't really want to be a doctor, nurse, lawyer, or engineer. My talents, interests, and goals didn't align with any of the careers my parents deemed acceptable. Their expectations were informed by their culture. Where they grew up, providing for your family with a stable income was one of the key reasons you worked. I understood where they were coming from. These careers offered stability, and these paths had been followed by many members of the society we are part of. Safety, predictability, and prestige were all benefits of pursuing one of these tried-and-true careers. As much as I tried to compromise, I decided to choose a different life for myself. I wanted to wait until I'd had a chance to explore my other options before committing to one career.

Ultimately, I discovered a loophole: if I gained admission into a highly selective university, my parents agreed to let me do whatever I wanted. I argued that if I could get that far, it had to indicate I was capable enough to be successful in whatever career I chose. So I put all my time and energy into college application season.

Applying to colleges is stressful for any young student, but I had always tempered my anxiety with the justification that I'd worked hard enough to get into at least one of my top-tier dream schools. I worked diligently during my entire academic career—performing at the top of my class while also leading various student organizations. I had prided myself not in my natural talents but in the hard work that led to the results I desired. For years, I had been told I could do whatever I wanted—my family, my peers, and my teachers supported me without fail. After all, my track record made us all confident in where my future could lead. Yet when I walked into my academic advisor's office that fall, he didn't even have to say a word before I felt my seeds of doubt take over. I could tell from the moment he read my preferred list of colleges that he didn't believe I would make it.

"Shana," he began gently, "these are all amazing colleges, but they're *really really* hard to get into. I just think it'd be better if you included less...competitive universities in your list."

It took a moment to gather my thoughts, and those few seconds seemed to stretch for an eternity. "But," I started in the same quiet tone, "I don't want to go anywhere else *but* these places."

I wasn't trying to be difficult, or even naïve. To me, these universities represented the chance to pursue my intellectual interests without being limited to one outstanding department or a specific program. I could confidently go to the university and believe I would study whatever I wanted and come out successful and well-prepared. As a young woman who dreamed of changing the world, I wanted to give myself the best possible chance for making it happen, and I knew it started with reaching the highest quality of education I could attain for myself. My driving force for the past twelve years of my academic career had been to continuously learn and push myself so I could attend any college I wanted.

He looked at me with a little pity, as if he'd had this conversation with multiple other high-achieving students in the past. "Yes, but you have to understand that they're almost all a stretch. I just want you to have options," he replied earnestly, and I could see that even though I didn't agree with him, he genuinely was coming from a good place. But when he said "options," it made me realize he didn't think I would get many of the offers I had been hoping for, *if any of them*.

In the moment, I couldn't comprehend what he'd said to me. *Look at my transcript!* I wanted to shout. *Look at all the activities I've done, my letters of recommendation, the positions I've held! Why isn't it enough?* But after a few seconds of awkward silence, I plastered on a smile and told him I'd reconsider my list and walked out quickly. I'd been trained to do this for years—*just smile and listen to what the adults tell you, Shana. You're too young, too naïve to understand how the real world works.* In that one instance, years of work were suddenly called into question. Maybe I *was* just too naïve, maybe I didn't understand my odds, maybe I couldn't bet on myself the way I thought I could.

While I didn't change my list, I couldn't shake the new sense of doubt that stuck around me. My applications suddenly seemed too daunting, and I halfheartedly completed many of them, picking majors my parents wanted and struggling to come up with genuine rationales for studying those subjects. I was self-sabotaging without fully realizing it, all because of one comment. Some people may think it was ridiculous to let it affect me so much, but it takes just one moment to completely change your view of yourself and your capabilities if you let it.

I became unsure of myself. When other people doubted my abilities, it made me wonder if I ever had them in the first place. I wasn't convinced my voice mattered. I didn't have any dramatic experiences to draw upon, nor did I have the money or resources to become the female changemaker I wanted to be. Was I even meant to be someone like Malala when we had nothing in common? But that was where I was wrong.

There are more similarities between people like Malala and me than I initially thought. We're both young women who have experienced hardships. We both come from cultures in which women are generally put down in a myriad of ways. We both had opportunities to be educated and come from supportive families, but many people in the world still don't wish to see us succeed. We both care about other young women and want to make changes that will positively impact populations for years to come. We both dream of a better world because we see ourselves in other young women struggling to create lives of stability, safety, comfort, and joy.

I've come to realize a simple truth: we are all Malala.

Anyone can be a changemaker. You just need the right tools: the correct mindset, access to resources, and a supportive environment. And while these may seem like predetermined factors one can't control, there are plenty of ways to create a path for yourself with the right guidance.

This book will serve as that tool, not only for young women but for any person wishing to support the women in their lives. Parents, siblings, grandparents, cousins, teachers, mentors, friends, your friendly coffee shop barista —so many people want to see women succeed but merely lack the knowledge of how to help. Through the stories I've collected, this book will help you learn to listen to your voice, find your support, and drive the change you want in the world.

These lessons were uncovered by drawing upon the stories of both well-known and under-the-radar female changemakers, all of whom are creating immeasurable impact. While they may appear to have nothing in common, I've discovered many similarities between their trajectories. You'll likely find yourself resonating with at least one of these women in some way because, at the crux of it all, they are normal people just like you and me.

Through their stories, I've discovered the core principles of what makes a successful female changemaker. I've done all the research for you, so now you have unrestricted access to the knowledge of which tools will help lift you up to where you want to go and why they're important.

You will realize you can do anything you put your mind to, and with the right tools and people around you, you can go further than you ever dreamed.

PART 1

HOW WE GOT HERE

"There is no force equal to a woman determined to rise."

—W. E. B. DUBOIS

CHAPTER 1

THE FEMALE EMPOWERMENT MOVEMENT

———

The future is female.

How often have you seen that slogan, slashed across t-shirts, social media posts, and brick walls? Many of us have noticed female empowerment has taken up a new momentum in modern society.[12] Now, more than ever, millions of people are attempting to fight not only for gender equality but for women to have the resources to thrive. But even though this

---

12   "Empowerment: A Multi-Dimensional Social Process That Helps People Gain Control over Their Own Lives. It Is a Process That Fosters Power in People for Use in Their Own Lives, Their Communities and in Their Society, by Acting on Issues They Define as Important," Nanette Page and Cheryl E. Czuba, "Empowerment: What Is It?" *Journal of Extension* 37, no.5 (1999).

slogan claims the future is female, what good is it if we forget that the past was also filled with females as well?

For thousands of years, women have been the backbone for societal function. It seems obvious, as they make up about half of the world's population, but much of their work goes unnoticed and/or under-appreciated. In fact, most of their efforts are *expected* of them; the gender norms many cultures depend on for distribution of power and tasks have gone unchanged for centuries.

How many young girls have been told to cultivate skills to be "marriage-ready" as their male counterparts were allowed to run free and wild outside, without a care in the world? How many women have been expected to perform back-breaking work at home, caring for children and the household in resource-scarce areas, without being given any respect and being under the constant threat of violence from their partners? How many women have been affected by the politics, laws, and customs of the places they live, yet are allowed no say in the decisions that concern their own bodies and lives?

The questions don't only stop at how many women *have* suffered, but how many women *continue* to suffer.

These questions may be enough for some, but others need more to answer the core query: why women? The world has survived this long with the current systems in place; in fact, it has even thrived and flourished in ways our ancestors could never have imagined, yet millions of men and women are struggling. So why invest in women specifically?

While I would never deny that assistance should be offered to all people in need, a plethora of data demonstrates the societal value of empowering women in particular. Women are seen as the centers of their communities and family units. They are often the main determinant of the health of their children, spouse, and extended relatives. According to the World Health Organization, cultural gender norms such as economic dependence and patriarchal structures create social dynamics that cause health barriers.[13] In other words, centuries of gender norms have created systems that prevent women from being their healthiest.

Many societal influences can block a woman's access to health information and services; for example, the universal tendency to burden women with a greater share of domestic responsibilities, yet simultaneously leaving them with little power over the resources they can use. In most cases, the women of the family are responsible for caring for those in their homes and communities, while men's responsibilities tend to fall outside the domestic sphere.

Empowering women benefits entire families. When economically empowered, mothers tend to use their earnings to invest in their children's education and health. According to the Clinton Global Initiative, women reinvest close to 90 percent of their incomes in their families, while men generally only reinvest 30 to 40 percent.[14] Since economically empowering a woman over a man likely ensures close to three times

13   "Gender," World Health Organization, accessed June 8, 2020.

14   "Empowering Girls and Women," Clinton Global Initiative, United Nations Economic and Social Council, accessed June 8, 2020.

the amount of reinvestment in communities, that statistic alone should be enough to encourage societies to provide more economic opportunities to their female citizens. When women can fully participate in economic activities, they can afford better food, shelter, clothing, health care, and more for their families.

With women being at the center of many societies, it's clear to see the relationship between empowering women and overall societal benefits. For any conceivable sector of society—economic, political, social, health, etc.—gender equality improves the outcomes of that sector significantly. However, even if ample research supports female empowerment, it continues to be an upward battle. Much of the current political and economic infrastructure in place does not account for the inclusion of women, let alone the rights they deserve. Many discriminatory practices continue throughout the world, whether concerning job opportunities, political representation, or cultural stereotypes and mindsets.

For some people who have been granted power and privilege in society, giving up even a small share of that power to move toward equality is unwanted. In many countries such as Egypt, Nicaragua, and the United States, millions of women are denied access to safe abortions.[15] In Yemen, women are considered only a half a witness in court when they testify.[16]

---

15   "The World's Abortion Laws," Center for Reproductive Rights, accessed June 8, 2020.

16   "Yemen: Women's Rights Must Be Front and Center," Amnesty International, accessed June 8, 2020.

In Vatican City, women are still unable to vote.[17] Many others ignore the evidence. They claim the data is falsified or has no true basis, saying things like "The gender wage gap doesn't exist" or "Women are too emotional to be effective leaders."

Unfortunately, even those in the highest positions of society will possess and express these ideas, even national leaders such as presidents. In the United States, women's right to vote doesn't guarantee them the respect of their elected leaders. Donald Trump tweeted in October 2019 that "Hillary's gone Crazy [sic]!" in response to her insinuating former Democratic presidential candidate Tulsi Gabbard and former Green Party presidential candidate Jill Stein were "Russian" assets.[18] By reinforcing the idea that she's gone "crazy," he was attempting to invalidate her opinions and ideas. While politics is notorious for candidates trading insults, politicians often attack their female counterparts by attributing their ideas to their emotions rather than leaning on factual counterarguments.

A survey conducted in 2019 revealed about four in ten Americans (38 percent) still believed the gender wage gap was made to serve political purposes, peaking at 46 percent among men.[19] When Georgetown University conducted a longitu-

17   Elisabetta Povoledo, "Vatican Faces Modern-Day Suffragists, Demanding Right to Vote," *The New York Times*, October 26, 2018.

18   Jason Murdock, "'Hillary's Gone Crazy': Trump Defends Tulsi Gabbard after Clinton Says Democratic Candidate Is Being 'Groomed' by Russia," *Newsweek*, October 10, 2019.

19   Jillesa Gebhardt, "On Equal Pay Day 2019, Lack of Awareness Persists," *Curiosity at Work (blog)*, Survey Monkey, accessed June 8, 2020.

dinal study from 1974–2018, it revealed that even though it has decreased over time, 13 percent of Americans still believe men are better suited emotionally for politics than most women today.[20] While these statistics may represent American attitudes specifically, these sentiments aren't limited to the United States. They're found everywhere.

Societies are, of course, welcome to hold onto the valued traditions of their cultures: the traditions that don't treat women poorly, that don't endanger their health and safety, that don't take away their voices, and don't diminish their chances at success and happiness. The world continues to change, and it is important to realize societies must change as humanity discovers new revelations and old truths: women were always meant to be valued and respected—and this means their rights and freedoms are non-negotiable.

As Phumzile Mlambo-Ngcuka, under-secretary-general of the United Nations and executive director of UN Women, stated at the IIFMENA conference in 2016, "Women and girls are not a burden or a charity case; they are resilient, they are solution-makers, and they can stand up for themselves. All they ask for is a chance."[21] This chance can change billions of lives and help societies reach heights we couldn't even begin to imagine.

---

20   Anthony P. Carnevale, Nicole Smith and Kathryn Peltier Campbell, "May the Best Woman Win? Education and Biases Against Women in American Politics," Georgetown University Center on Education and the Workforce, 2019.

21   Phumzile Mlambo-Ngcuka, "Women oooooooo," UN Women, October 20, 2016.

WHY DO WOMEN STILL HESITATE?

Across the globe, women are stuck in resource-scarce areas. Even if they have the intention and drive to empower themselves, without the proper resources, it is difficult to change their lives in the ways they want. A prominent example is the lack of access to clean water and sanitation facilities in various regions of Africa. The Water Project, a non-profit dedicated to providing reliable water projects to communities in Sub-Saharan Africa, details how the insufficient number of safe water sources can create a cycle of poverty that is difficult to break. It also presents extra challenges for young girls.

Since fetching water is typically a woman's responsibility in these communities, it limits their access to education and business opportunities. According to The Water Project, "Every day, women and young girls carry more than forty pounds of dirty water from sources over four miles away from their homes."[22] The hours needed to make this journey on a daily basis leave little time to make education a priority, continuing the poverty cycle with little hope for improvement without an intervention. When considering situations like these, it's easy to see why women may be unable to make the changes they desire. Without the right infrastructure in place, it's hard enough to survive on a daily basis, let alone strive for a better life.

But what about the women who aren't stuck in those areas? The women who have access to the proper support network,

22   "The Water Crisis: Education in Africa," The Water Project, accessed June 8, 2020.

resources, and live in societies in which many other women have changed their lives and the lives of others? Why do women still hesitate to make a change, even if they are given the tools to do so?

As various bodies of research shows, no sole reason causes this hesitation. Rather, a group of different factors work together to keep women from pursuing the goals they desire.

THE GENDER CONFIDENCE GAP

One such reason is the gender confidence gap. In the past several years, various studies have demonstrated women tend to underestimate their skill level, intelligence, and personal value when compared to men. This leads them to refrain from seeking opportunities, negotiating higher salaries, or even fighting for their rights.

According to an internal report done by Hewlett-Packard several years ago, women only applied for new jobs when they met 100 percent of the criteria, while men applied even if they only met 60 percent.[23] Other studies done at Yale, UC Santa Barbara, Cornell, Washington State, and other universities all mimic similar results of women underestimating themselves, whether on test scores, value to organizations, or professional competency.[24]

---

23 Nancy F. Clark, "Act Now to Shrink the Confidence Gap," *Forbes*, April 28, 2014.

24 Katty Kay and Claire Shipman, "The Confidence Gap," *The Atlantic*, May 2014.

Whereas women tend to underestimate themselves, men tend to do the complete opposite: they will happily overestimate their abilities. Ernesto Reuben, a Columbia Business School professor, coined the simple term *honest overconfidence.*[25] Men aren't immune to self-doubt; they simply don't let doubt hinder them from seeking out new opportunities. It seems they naturally fall toward overconfidence, as they aren't consciously trying to fool others.

To illustrate this idea, Reuben conducted a study in 2011 which showed men rated their test performance 30 percent better than it actually was.[26] In study after study, the same result occurs: men are always overconfident and, therefore, rate themselves based on their belief in their own abilities. If men can do it, wouldn't the answer to this issue be to tell women to believe in themselves more?

Unfortunately, the magic solution can't be to just "fake it 'til you make it." False confidence can only get you so far, and even then, it is not as potent as true overconfidence. In most settings, it's not necessarily the most intelligent or most capable person that draws the crowd's attention and support; it's the most self-assured. This is because humans also count on non-verbal cues as well.

According to an interview done by *The Atlantic* with Cameron Anderson, a psychologist who works at UC Berkeley, these self-assured people tend to use expansive body language, a lower vocal tone, often speak early, and speak in a relaxed

---

25   Ibid.

26   Ibid.

manner.[27] These cues alert others they are confident in their abilities and, therefore, exude dependability to their peers. If a woman doesn't truly believe in her capabilities, it becomes more difficult for her to exude the same verbal and non-verbal cues, and her likelihood of gaining the same respect and social status granted to a truly overconfident man is slim.

Impostor syndrome is a common diagnosis for such lack of confidence. It's the false and potentially crippling belief that one's successes are the product of luck or fraud rather than skill.[28] While any person can feel such a way, Facebook's chief operating officer, Sheryl Sandberg, believes women experience it more intensely and are more limited by it.[29] In her book *Lean In*, she recounts how every time she "didn't embarrass [herself]—or even excelled," she believed she had fooled the people around her.[30]

Sandberg is objectively a very capable and successful woman; it takes hard work and talent to become the COO of one of the most successful companies in the world. Yet she demonstrates no woman is immune to such doubts; it can negatively affect them if they let it control their lives and decisions. When women believe they don't deserve to be where they are, it leads them to restrict themselves from flourishing in their chosen paths. In fact, it's often found that women tend to internalize their struggles rather than their successes.

---

27   Ibid.

28   *Merriam-Webster*, s.v., "Impostor Syndrome (*n.*)," accessed June 8, 2020.

29   Sheryl Sandberg, *Lean In: Women, Work, and the Will to Lead* (New York, New York: Random House Audio, 2013), 28.

30   Ibid.

INTERNAL ATTRIBUTION VERSUS EXTERNAL ATTRIBUTION

Internalizing struggles is another common trait of women that promotes hesitancy to make a change. Whenever women struggle and/or fail, they tend to attribute the failure to their own inability. Men, on the other hand, tend to externally attribute rather than take all the blame for themselves. For example, in the PhD math program at Cornell, one course is often very difficult for the candidates.

David Dunning, a psychologist at the university, states that the male students tend to recognize the difficulty for what it is: a difficult class.[31] They understand their lower grades are a result of the class being unavoidably difficult for most, which, in this situation, is considered a healthy resilience factor. However, Dunning then noticed that when the female students received their lower grades, they attributed the grades to "not being good enough." Their internal attributions could prove to be debilitating later in the program and, more importantly, in life.

BIOLOGICAL/DEVELOPMENT BASIS

This propensity does have biological roots. Male and female brains are more alike than different, but some differences may cause women to lean toward being more hesitant. The areas of the female brain are more centered to worry and remembering negative events—in layman's terms, they have a larger "worrywart" center. Also, the presence of estrogen

31   "Overconfident Men," *Utah Women and Leadership Project (blog)*, Utah Valley University, August 27, 2015.

promotes the need for bonding and connection, which dissuades women from risk and conflict. Testosterone, on the other hand, chases the "winner effect." It encourages aggression, risk taking, and demonstrations of power.[32]

The way children are raised will lead to their eventual confidence or hesitation. As children, girls are rewarded for being "good" (i.e. well-behaved, good listeners, obedient) while boys are allowed to be rambunctious, pushy, etc., with the excuse that "boys will be boys." Girls also tend to get a lot of praise for being perfect; they're more easily socialized as they have "longer attention spans, they have further advanced verbal and motor skills, and greater social adeptness." They are rewarded for doing things "neatly and quietly," which almost promotes the idea that women shouldn't draw attention to their accomplishments.[33]

Even punishments can be influential in how women are perceived. When boys get written up for bad behavior, it's often attributed to a lack of effort. Young girls, however, often see these instances as about their inner qualities. They believe they are not capable, they are not intelligent, they aren't nice enough.[34] If risk taking, failure, and perseverance lead to confidence, how can girls develop such an essential quality if they don't get to explore such things based on social tailoring?

32   Kay and Shipman, "The Confidence Gap," 2014.

33   Ibid.

34   Ibid.

THE BACKLASH EFFECT

But what about when women decide to go forward confidently in their abilities? Even this can lead to negative consequences. Due to the backlash effect, or the social and economic reprisals for behaving counter-stereotypically, women can get "punished" for not conforming to gender stereotypes, being perceived as less likable or less hirable. According to a 2008 study, women are often perceived as less competent, ambitious, and competitive than men.[35] This causes them to be overlooked for leadership positions unless they present themselves as what is considered an "atypical woman."

Research shows women receive a higher social and professional penalty for being perceived as aggressive, while men tend to be rewarded for such behavior.[36] Not just competence is called into question but a woman's character as well. This causes women to have to simultaneously be two things at once: they must be kind and have a high pro-social orientation, yet also be confident and assertive. It's a delicate balance. If too confident, they are perceived as aggressive, but if too modest, they will be overlooked. Women constantly must qualify that they use their assertiveness to benefit others, or else they run the risk of negative social and professional consequences.

The fear of the backlash effect itself can lead women to behave differently at all stages of their careers. Northern Illinois

---

35   Laurie A. Rudman and Julie E. Phelan, "Backlash Effects for Disconfirming Gender Stereotypes in Organizations," *Research in Organizational Behavior* 28, (2008), 61-79.

36   Ibid.

University conducted a study where female students had to write essays explaining why they are deserving and worthy recipients of a scholarship.[37] Part of the group was told it would be done anonymously, while the other part was told their name would be attached to the application. When asked to rate their performance, the anonymous writers were more likely to rate their achievements higher, as they didn't have to worry about any backlash.

Victoria Brescoll from the Yale School of Management conducted several studies demonstrating how women in higher leadership positions state they will speak less than male CEOs, as they don't wish to be "disliked" or "out of line."[38] Both genders rate women more negatively for talking more. Even if men speak for the same amount of time, they don't get rated as poorly. In fact, a female CEO described as talking less than others had a higher perceived competency.

With all these consequences for a woman's behavior, it becomes clear why there are so many challenges to a woman's success. It's almost paralyzing in a sense; how do you act if everything you do is scrutinized, and the very actions that should theoretically help you have the potential to backfire?

Yet staying in the same place and refusing to act will never lead to better conditions. Inaction breeds low confidence— if they don't even attempt to succeed, women already set

---

37   Meghan I. H. Lindeman, Amanda M. Durik, and Maura Dooley, "Women and Self-Promotion: A Test of Three Theories," *Psychological Reports* 122, no. 1 (2019): 219-230.

38   Kay and Shipman, "The Confidence Gap," 2014.

themselves up for failure. To build a sense of self-efficacy, women need to take action. Rather than fearing failure at the get-go, it's more valuable to try and fail rather than hold back and never pursue anything. The more action taken, the greater confidence in ability is cultivated.

When Lucía Berro Pizzarossa moved from rural Uruguay to its capital of Montevideo, the last thing she thought she'd discover was a passion for reproductive and sexual rights. Yet in the capital city, she understood how gender inequality was hindering women from participating democratically. With abortion being illegal in the past, she couldn't believe women were denied ownership over their own bodies and lives. If that was the case, how would they be heard in the political realm if political figures didn't think they deserved to make decisions for their *own* lives? In an interview, Pizzarossa laughs when she recalls her parents' reaction when she decided to pursue human rights. "They thought I was crazy because it wasn't a 'conventional' degree, but I was stubborn and stayed true to my path."

Battling for reproductive and sexual rights is difficult throughout the world, and the machismo culture that specifically plagues Latin America intensifies an imbalance of power between the genders. But Pizzarossa stayed true to her mission, pursuing higher education, and is currently a network and partnerships coordinator for the Mobilizing Activists for Medical Abortion Network, as well as a post-doctoral researcher at the Global Health Law Groningen Research Centre. She is now responsible for preparing briefs on international laws and informing decisions on sexual and reproductive health and rights, and uses her knowledge to strengthen campaigns and develop litigation to further her cause. But as you may guess, the journey to get to where she is now wasn't always smooth sailing.

A few years ago, Pizzarossa pursued the opportunity to go to Oxford for research and further studies, but she had yet another battle to fight as she stepped on campus. As she walked into meetings, people constantly tried to pin a narrative on her. She was suddenly the "poor rural Latina woman who somehow made it," but Lucía had never even considered herself poor until she stepped onto Oxford's campus. Sure, she had grown up on a farm and rode horses to school, but everyone in her community did that. Either way, she found her youth to be very fulfilling because, in her eyes, her parents had given her everything she could've wanted. She quickly realized that, in the field of research and academia, no large Latina presence existed in Oxford, so people simply pushed the narrative that worked with their idea of the world.

When I asked Lucía how she felt about this, she didn't hide her irritation. "I refuse to look back at my life and assess it to [their] categories," she stated frankly. "I never saw myself as underprivileged! By what measures had they come to that conclusion—according to the standards of capitalism and materialism?"

To mitigate the issue, she emphasized the importance of reclaiming your story, especially as a young woman of color. When she walked into meetings, or was introduced to others, she made sure to inform people of her own perspective on her life. Rather than focus on her upbringing, she pointed out her hardworking nature and fierce passion as the conductors of her success. "Do not let other people tell your story or narrate who you are," she emphasized. She stressed one should not be defined by other people's stories about you; it often is a tactic used to ignore or invalidate the important characteristics that got you to where you are.

Pizzarossa implores women to take action because she understands the danger of not acting at all. "Don't give up," she says. "The journey will not be easy, and you're working in a system that is designed to a certain extent to not take your voice into consideration. But try many different things, and if something doesn't suit you, take a break and then get up to try again." She related that inaction only favors the status quo, so it's important to be proactive and fight for the greater good in whatever way you choose.

Lucía is just one of the many women who have chosen to act. Millions of women still need help gaining this momentum. Female empowerment doesn't just require the effort of the women in need—factors at every level and sector of life contribute to the empowerment of women. From child development, corporate attitudes, political representation, and health resource dissemination, there is no shortage of ways to change the narratives that have kept women from reaching their highest potential.

We must recognize that we need to make a change.

CHAPTER 2

THE HISTORY OF SOCIAL CHANGE

———

When I was a girl growing up just outside Chicago, I started dreaming I would somehow, someday, do something great and change the world. Perhaps you've had that dream too. Did we even understand what change is?

Change. We hear this broad term thrown around in speeches, lectures, presentations, and song lyrics, but it can be interpreted differently based on the situation and perspective of the person speaking. For our purposes, the specific type of change encouraged throughout this book is social change.

According to *Encyclopaedia Britannica*, social change (from a sociological perspective) is "the alteration of mechanisms within the social structure, characterized by changes in cultural symbols, rules of behavior, social organizations, or value systems."[39] This type of change can stem from various sources, such as diffusion through contact with other societies; changes in the ecosystem due to natural disasters or the spread of diseases; technological change; population growth and changes in demographics; and ideological, economic, and political movements.

As the saying goes, "The only constant in life is change." Both short-term and small-scale changes are an intrinsic aspect of human society, as customs and norms adapt to new techniques and technologies as they are invented. Adaptations result from environmental changes, and power is redistributed as conflicts rise and fall between societies. Change is unavoidable because humans are biologically primed to have the potential for change. As humans, we have various fixed action patterns, or instincts, but we also have an enormous capacity for learning and creating. While social change can be stimulated through the virtue of the biological traits of humanity, the nature of the actual changes can't be solely attributed to these qualities.

Social change emerges from a variety of sources, ranging from natural disasters to globalization to population trends. For example, the increase in population density in a country may stimulate innovations in technology, which could increase the division of labor, commercialization, social differentiation, and/or economic stagnation. However, one of the most powerful instigators of social change is very simple: an idea.

---

39 *Encyclopaedia Britannica Online*, Academic ed., s.v., "Social Change,"
    by William Form and Nick Wilterdink, accessed June 8, 2020.

The transformation of collective ideas is not just a mental process; this exchange creates new social movements, especially when combined with what nineteenth-century sociologist Max Weber called "charismatic leadership." This type of leader has a set of extraordinary personal characteristics that lead to the creation of a group of followers willing to break the established rules of society.[40] Charisma is subjective, but regardless, those considered charismatic can do immense good for society or commit great evils.

Social processes intertwine with other aspects of society; separating these factors would overlook the combinations of influences that stimulate such processes. Just as no fixed borders exist between economic and political processes or between economy and technology, social processes can originate from any sector of society too. As these connections form over time, it can be difficult to distinguish these developments from their respective origin points. But you've got to start somewhere. And if any group is perfect for catalyzing progress, it's the demographic most discredited by society: our youth.

Young people can be the driving forces of change. Before you doubt them, hear me out. They aren't naïve, impressionable children anymore. By the time they've exited their teens, many have dealt with trials, tragedy, loss, indescribable pain, and other hardships, and they've come out on the other side more resilient. These young adults have cultivated an elevated

---

40   *The Stanford Encyclopedia of Philosophy*, Winter 2019 ed., s.v., "Max
      Weber," by Sung Ho Kim, edited by Edward N. Zalta, accessed on June
      8, 2020.

sense of knowledge on a variety of subjects. Among this group are hard workers, go-getters, and empathetic friends. Rather than discredit them due to their youth, their youth provides many reasons why they are perfect for creating social change. In fact, they're already creating it.[41]

Today's youth is also unconstrained by how things should be. Many have little attachment to *how things are supposed to be* and would rather see the world for what it *could* be. They have grown up in a world that is changing and developing more rapidly than ever before, and they envision how things could be changed for the better. The things that were once impossible are now parts of daily life, so what's to say their dreams cannot one day be a reality?

When you're constantly growing and experiencing new things all the time, you'll typically become accustomed to learning new things. Young people are used to learning and adapting information and may feel less obliged to pretend they know everything. They're open to exploring new ideas, making them ideal candidates for involvement in social movements. They question and digest information quickly to apply it to the problems they encounter. These critical thinking skills prove invaluable when creating social change, as they seek to explore what they don't understand and strive to find ways to apply what they know to real life.

I truly realized exactly how powerful young people could be in my college years. My peers are starting businesses,

---

41   Rachel Cain, "Five Reasons to Be Cheerful About Young People and Social Change," *Sheila McKechnie Foundation*, March 19, 2019.

innovating solutions for pressing issues, and helping execute health initiatives in other countries. They have a fire and passion that hasn't been dimmed by reality and run themselves ragged to support the causes they care about. They'll pour their time, energy, blood, sweat, and tears into everything they do just to get one step closer to fulfilling their personal missions. I'd never felt more motivated to do the same until I'd seen how much impact my friends were making in their respective spheres. Everywhere I look, people my age are stepping up and rising to the challenges many others discard.

Some may try to use their youth against them, but being relatively inexperienced in this world is valuable. Due to their youth, many young people have yet to become desensitized to injustices. They don't feel they should merely accept this suffering as part of life. Rather, they are appalled and want to strive to right the many wrongs that plague our world.

When I started talking about how I wanted to work with vulnerable populations, and even potentially abroad, people constantly attributed my youth as the reason my dreams would be dashed. *This is just how the world is, Shana. You can't help everyone. You're too young to understand what it's really like out there.*

Sure, I will never be able to solve every problem or save every person in the world. There will be issues I could never predict, struggles I'll have to go through, and many low points that will probably make me contemplate whether I made the right decision in pursuing a life of advocacy and global health innovation. But I can't accept a life of just sitting around and accepting our reality when I know I could be part of the movement that changes that reality. Regardless of whether I'm successful, I *will* regret it if I never even try—and luckily for our world, millions of young people share this sentiment.

Globally, young people are usually more optimistic and energetic than their older counterparts. The Bill and Melinda Gates Foundation's Goalkeeper's Global Youth Poll discovered most young people believe their generation will have a positive impact on the world.[42] It may be because many of them have yet to be jaded by life, or they may not completely understand the complexity of the issues they face, but no one can deny young people have a unique energy. This energy promotes resilience, and if tapped into correctly, it's possible to have millions of young people working toward a cause throughout the world if engaged properly.

While young people may be constantly underestimated, throughout history, they've been the driving force behind countless social movements across the world. No matter what country or decade you examine, young people have never chosen to rest on the sidelines in the face of injustice. On the contrary, they tend to be the ones at the forefront of protests and are often the most vocal and active in advocating for change.

For example, take the Civil Rights Movement in America— one of the most iconic social movements in modern history.

---

42   "Gates Foundation Poll Finds Young People More Optimistic about Future Than Older Generations; Optimism Highest in Lower- and Middle-Income Countries," *Bill and Melinda Gates Foundation*, September 24, 2018.

This struggle took place just over sixty years ago, which makes it fairly recent in the grand scheme of social justice. In this era, young people were instrumental to the success of the movement. They were both visible in active protests, such as lunch counter sit-ins, and also incredibly involved behind the scenes when organizing countless efforts.[43]

The Student Nonviolent Coordinating Committee (SNCC) was incredibly influential, embracing non-violent protest tactics and educating and training many of the young advocates who worked for the movement.[44] Challenging segregated schools, racism, and voter disenfranchisement, they endured physical violence, state repression, and constant harassment as they tirelessly organized various efforts on a multitude of fronts.[45] In fact, it was once the largest and most well-organized civil rights group, which demonstrates the power young people can have when mobilized.[46]

It didn't just stop at domestic struggles either—the Vietnam War mobilized thousands upon thousands of people as well. During the Vietnam War, over two million young men were drafted into the U.S. military.[47] As a result, it was inevitable

---

43 Ibid.

44 *Encyclopaedia Britannica Online*, Academic ed., s.v., "Montgomery Bus Boycott to the Voting Rights Act," by Clayborne Carson, accessed on June 8, 2020.

45 Charlie Cobb, "Challenging White Power," *SNCC Digital Gateway*, accessed on June 8, 2020.

46 Ibid.

47 University of Michigan, "The Military Draft During the Vietnam War," *Michigan in the World*, accessed on June 8, 2020.

that young people were to be at the heart of the protests against the war. This movement led by the students influenced the American public to turn against the war. They marched, conducted sit-ins, and continuously agitated the public against the war.[48] They ended up dividing the country on whether they should be allowed to protest or needed to be stopped.

In some cases, such as the Kent State University demonstration in 1970, unarmed students were tear-gassed, hassled, and even killed by the police.[49] Some groups, such as the Students for Democratic Society, were scrutinized by the FBI for their anti-war efforts.[50] Yet they persisted, understanding silence would not produce conversation. They understood the controversy would create debate and discussion to instigate the change they desired.

When thinking about movements that shook the globe, the one that often comes to mind is the Tiananmen Square protests of 1989. The protest wasn't a one-off event that turned into the horrible massacre that killed hundreds to thousands of unarmed demonstrators.[51] It was one of many protests

---

48   "Vietnam War Protests," *A&E Television Networks*, accessed June 8, 2020.

49   Jerry M. Lewis and Thomas R. Hensley, "The May 4 Shootings at Kent State University: The Search for Historical Accuracy," *Kent State University*, accessed June 8, 2020.

50   William W. Riggs, "Students for a Democratic Society," *The First Amendment Encyclopedia – Middle Tennessee State University*, accessed June 8, 2020.

51   "Tiananmen Square Protests," *A&E Television Networks*, accessed June 8, 2020.

led by the youth, demanding democratic reform and economic liberalization after years of attempted reforms that only benefited some while disproportionately negatively affecting others.[52]

The protests were driven by the anxiety of the country's future, and the students demanded their basic freedoms to be granted (i.e. freedom of the press, speech, constitutional due process).[53] At the height of the demonstration, close to a million people had gathered.[54] To this day, China continues to censor the information about the attack, yet these young people's impact will continue as their legacy for many years to come.[55]

While I wish that change could be initiated without violence being the catalyst, it goes without saying that many horrible things have led to great changes. In 2011, Mohammed Bouazizi, a Tunisian street vendor, committed suicide by self-immolation.[56] This was not a random event but a protest against the forcible shutdown of his shop and the harassment he had suffered from the police. His death catalyzed an unprecedented revolution called the Arab Spring. A series of

52 Ibid.

53 "Timeline: What Led to the Tiananmen Square Massacre," *FRONTLINE Newsletter*, PBS, WGBH Educational Foundation, accessed June 10, 2020.

54 "Tiananmen Square: What Happened in the Protests of 1989?" *BBC News*, accessed on June 10, 2020.

55 James Griffiths, "World Marks 30 Years Since Tiananmen Massacre as China Censors All Mention," *CNN*, June 4, 2019.

56 *Encyclopaedia Britannica Online*, Academic ed., s.v., "Mohamed Bouazizi," accessed on June 10, 2020.

pro-democracy protests and uprisings took place across the Middle East, spreading from Tunisia to Egypt, Libya, Yemen, Syria, and more.[57]

The youth, frustrated by human rights violations, police corruption, and oppressive regimes, took to the streets and turned public plazas into protest hubs, where the struggle gained visibility.[58] Cairo's Tahir Square was the center of huge protests for eighteen days, drawing tens of thousands of Egyptians demanding their president, Hosni Mubarak, step down.[59] They eventually got the president of thirty years out of office, which led to a period of political instability. While the country attempts to continually repress its citizens, analysts such as M. Chloe Mulderig of Boston University believe the youth's impetus was key. In an interview with National Geographic, she says that Arab Spring "could not have occurred without the ideological and numerical push of a huge mass of angry youth."[60]

The youth often aren't angry for no reason; they're angry at the injustices they face and the lack of response from those in positions of power. One of the most recent social movements has been the March for Our Lives movement to end gun

57   *Encyclopaedia Britannica Online*, Academic ed., s.v., "Arab Spring," accessed on June 10, 2020.

58   Erin Blakemore, "What Was the Arab Spring and How Did It Spread?" *National Geographic*, March 29, 2019.

59   Yolanda Knell, "Egypt's revolution: 18 days in Tahrir Square," *BBC News*, January 25, 2012.

60   Erin Blakemore, "Youth in Revolt: Five Powerful Movements Fueled by Young Activists," *National Geographic*, March 23, 2018.

violence in America.[61] On February 14, 2018, a nineteen-year-old gunman walked into Marjory Stoneman Douglas High School in Parkland, Florida, and killed seventeen students and staff members.[62] This massacre would lead to one of the most powerful youth-led social movements in decades, and it started with twenty students who decided gun violence, now more than ever, needed to end.

March for Our Lives refused to let the media sweep the incident under the rug as one of several gun violence incidences and coined the hashtag #NeverAgain to implore political representatives to take the issue seriously. Emma Gonzalez, who became the face of the movement due to her iconic "We Call BS" speech, demonstrated with raw intensity that the issue of gun violence needed to be addressed with more than empty promises.[63] Within five weeks of the massacre, they organized the first rally in Washington, D.C., which drew over 800,000 participants and inspired similar protests in hundreds of cities across the globe.[64]

What is the point of looking back at all these movements? Even for me, a student who loves learning, I used to fight to

61 Maggie Jones, "The March for Our Lives Activists Showed Us How to Find Meaning in Tragedy," *Smithsonian Magazine*, December 2018.

62 Elizabeth Chuck, Alex Johnson, and Corky Siemaszko, "17 Killed in Mass Shooting at High School in Parkland, Florida," *NBC News*, February 14, 2019.

63 Ibid.

64 Rebecca Shabad, Chelsea Bailey, and Phil McCausland, "At March for Our Lives, Survivors Lead Hundreds of Thousands in Call for Change," *NBC News*, March 24, 2018.

keep myself awake during history lectures because it fell out of my area of interest. I was interested in the present and the future. The past is over, so wouldn't our time be better spent focusing on the days to come? We're a different generation, with different ideas, privileges, and stories of our own. Was it relevant to spend years learning how many wars and protests and issues humanity has fought over?

Through the eyes of the young woman I've become, I've started connecting the dots and realizing we shouldn't be disregarding the past, because it often influences our future. Years ago, I took a women's history class, where I learned about American women's issues throughout the past few centuries. I analyzed resources from the perspectives of the women involved rather than those who wrote about them. Suddenly, history meant a lot more to me because I connected with those I read about as *people*. I could see myself, my peers, and the same issues we witness today within their stories. History became more real, and I found that if I didn't look at the past, I would never fully understand how our current world came to be.

These historic events are more than just stories; they're the lifeblood of our society. We can't move forward without acknowledging our past, because if we don't do so, we may continue to make the same mistakes. Our experiences shape our reality, and if we refuse to take the time to see how generations have influenced and fought for the world we have today, how do we expect to do the same in the future? And when I finally took the time to look back at how far we've come, I can now find parts of myself in the people who fought for the things they cared about.

Considering the impact, heart, and effort of these young people throughout history, it would be difficult to invalidate the power mobilized young people can have. The movements that have created the biggest changes and drawn the most attention have all had the common factor of passionate young people willing to band together in a display of strength and unity.

CHAPTER 3

THE POWER OF TECHNOLOGY

Have you ever been awakened by a loud noise in the middle of the night? I don't mean the sound of your dog barking at the wind or a family member snoring next to you. I mean the bone-chilling sound of something so fierce and unfamiliar that your brain sends a fight, flight, or freeze signal throughout your body. In my case, it prompted me to look under my bed and in my closet before realizing I'm a grown woman and no longer afraid of monsters. That night, though, I sat in bed startled as the sound of growling swept through our household. Knowing I couldn't go to sleep without figuring out where it was coming from, I threw back the covers and forced myself out of my bed.

Bleary-eyed, I slowly inched down the stairs, avoiding the creakiest steps and barely breathing to keep from making a sound. Every second that passed made my heart beat faster. As I crept closer to the family room, the roars started resounding through the house, growing louder at an alarming rate.

Unsure of what I'd find, I protected myself in the only ways I could in the moment: dialing 911 and praying to a higher power. Making the sign of the cross, I slowly peeked over the cabinets to finally reveal...

My dad. Seated in front of his computer. Watching a *lion documentary.*

He had a blanket wrapped around himself, hair going in every direction, and his eyes were captivated by the animals on the screen in front of him. When I spotted his headphones over his ears, I trailed the cord to realize he'd left them unplugged. Simultaneously relieved and irritated, I stalked over to my dad, looking him dead in the eyes as I turned the volume down from 75 to 20 and plugged in the cord pointedly. Finally taking note of me, he innocently looked at me with wide eyes. "What are you doing up so late?" he asked.

"You've got to be kidding me, Dad." Too tired to argue about it, I sighed, rolled my eyes, and went back to bed, this time without the sounds of lions hunting in the background.

It's crazy how much technology can affect us. My dad is ecstatic that he can learn from people all over the world and constantly is watching documentaries on every topic under the sun, from wild animals to ancient history. But I can hardly believe I almost died of a heart attack because our speakers had convinced me a wild animal had come into our house and would eat me in the middle of the night. Nightmares aside, I couldn't imagine a life without my dad constantly showing me his new discoveries on the internet, or a life where a simple Google search couldn't answer almost every question I've ever thought of.

For most of us born in Generation Z, modern technology has been a part of our lives for so long, it's hard to remember life without it. With new advancements to phones, computers, and the hundreds of other gadgets at our disposal being released on a weekly basis, it's difficult to imagine what society used to be like without the world at our fingertips. While many generations are familiar with computers in general, there remains a large group of people unfamiliar with the expansiveness of the internet and its capabilities.

But while technology has been normalized as a part of daily life, it's vital to remember just how powerful it truly is. This global generation has tools that no previous generation could have ever imagined. And just as with any other sector of life, technology has forever altered the way social movements are run.

In the past, movements depended heavily on messages being spread through word of mouth and printed publications. These methods limited knowledge to a local level, and it would take at least hours, if not days and weeks, to spread the news of current events.

Previously, access to communication methods was controlled by the few people in power, or it was only accessible to certain segments of society.[65] The digital divide continues to

---

65   M. Usman Mirza et al., "Technology-Driven Inequality Leads to Poverty and Resource Depletion," *Ecological Economics* 160, no. 1 (June 2016): 215-226.

affect people, restricted in their ability to access, buy, and/ or use computers and the internet due to financial reasons, government censorship, or other social determinants.[66] The divide tends to affect those in developing countries and low-income communities the most, further disadvantaging those populations.

However, though the digital divide is still present and the problem needs to be addressed, the number of internet users across the world is now over 50 percent, or close to 4.1 billion people.[67] While the internet must continue to expand in its accessibility, it has come a long way since it first launched. The rise of social media has diversified how protests can gain momentum and has expanded the avenues in which news can be spread. Issues that once were limited to local communities can now gain traction on an international level.

Before technology played a big role in our daily lives, movements were executed based on organized group efforts. The National Women's Party in the early 1910s relied on many different tactics to push their mission for woman's suffrage in the United States. According to a Library of Congress document, they used "relentless lobbying, creative publicity stunts, repeated acts of nonviolent confrontation, and examples of civil disobedience" to draw attention to their mission.[68] These actions often gained the attention of news-

---

66   "The Digital Divide," Stanford University, accessed June 8, 2020.

67   "Statistics," International Telecommunications Union, United Nations, accessed June 8, 2020.

68   "Tactics and Techniques of the National Woman's Party Suffrage Campaign," Library of Congress, accessed June 8, 2020.

papers, which supplemented their word-of-mouth efforts and spread information across the country, even if it was slower.[69]

With all the technological advancements of today, disseminating information to large populations is easier than ever. Now, in an instant, you can share with the world something that happened mere seconds ago, with media such as videos and pictures, using only a few taps on your phone. These posts can be seen by thousands of people by the minute, creating a reach far more widespread than ever before.

Videos and photos can now be used as evidence of injustices, and even though they may be removed by authorities or platforms, tens of thousands of people are likely to witness the event by the time it disappears. Millions of strangers who never would have known about you can now choose to actively follow your online presence and keep up with your updates.

Various academics have noted how technology and social media have elevated our society's ability to create community. When inquiring about the positives of digital life, research showed social media presents the chance to find the people who share our passions, concerns, and interests, without being limited by time or geography. Academics have explained how the resources and perspectives of thousands of other people are available on the internet. Even advocates for social change can manage the scope of their impact, as

---

69   Ibid.

with technology, their potential reach can be expanded far past what it used to be.[70]

New methods of protests and activism have emerged from the influence of social media. From tweet-activism to "hacktivism," and more, you can use the online world to your advantage in many ways. According to a study done on social change in Africa, social media platforms are now considered "amplifiers" that can be used to lift up voices and educate others.[71] Technology can connect with people globally that have the resources you need and share your interests. Through the internet, you can find donors, fellow advocates, researchers, companies, etc.—anyone you need to advance your cause, you can find. They don't even have to be in your physical vicinity either, as countless supporters come from every corner of the world.

In fact, Africtivists, a pan-African advocate network, used the internet to network with other social movements across the world, supporting local cyber-activists with their various advocacy campaigns in countries such as Senegal, Cameroon, and Gambia. Collaborating with Internet Without Borders, they launched a crowdsourcing campaign to raise funds for a Virtual Private Network for Chadian activists in response

---

70   Janna Anderson and Lee Rainie, "The Positives of Digital Life," Pew Research Center, July 3, 2018.

71   Charles Vandyck and Ngnaoussi Elongue Cédric Christian, "Social Movement and Social Change in Africa," *WACSERIES Op-Ed*, West African Civil Society Institute, April 3, 2019.

to the internet and social network censorship by the government in 2018.[72]

It's become easier than ever to mobilize people with the rise of social media campaigns. If given unrestricted access to the internet, someone can demonstrate their stance on an issue, sharing information and stories to the networks they are a part of. While cyber-activism will never replace traditional forms of protest, such as rallies and petitions, it does provide an opportunity to reinforce collective identity and build solidarity. Below are just a few of the many campaigns that gained immense traction through technology/social media:

- #NeverAgain – As mentioned earlier, the March for Our Lives organization created this hashtag to raise awareness of the need to end gun violence. It has been added to over 1.8 million posts on Instagram and was part of hundreds of millions of tweets and impressions on Twitter. These two simple words spread a profound message and were one reason millions of people participated in various protests throughout the world.[73]
- Afrika Youth Movement – Through digital activism, they led a global campaign that canceled the death sentence of Noura Hussein, a young Sudanese teenager who had been condemned because she had stabbed her husband for attempting to rape her. They used apps such as WhatsApp and Facebook to disseminate information on her case

---

72 Isabelle Mayault, "How a Pan-African Network of Cyber Activists Has Been Strengthening Democracy Online," Quartz Africa, June 2, 2018.

73 Erin Gallagher, "#MarchForOurLives & #NeverAgain," Medium, March 25, 2018.

status in Sudan, which helped the case gain a following and pressure the government into revoking her sentence.[74]

- The 2019–2020 Hong Kong protests were triggered by the introduction of an unpopular bill that would allow extraditions to mainland China. Thousands of people have been protesting the bill, and soon videos showed how authorities were using excessive force on protesters, including releasing tear gas and rubber bullets on tens of thousands of people. As the videos circulated across various social media platforms, they led to global coverage of the protests, condemning the officials for their actions. Without these videos, many people around the world likely wouldn't have known the extent of the issues plaguing the city.[75]

- "Anti-Muslim" Law in India – India has recently passed a law that grants citizenship to religious minorities, except for Muslims, from neighboring countries. Legal experts have said it violates the country's secular constitution, as Muslims account for nearly 15 percent of the population. The response to the ban has been massive, with thousands of people protesting.[76] Since the law was passed, there have been videos recording the suffering of Muslims, including police beating protesters and unarmed civilians.[77] These videos have helped raise awareness of

74 "About Us," Afrika Youth Movement, accessed June 8, 2020.

75 Mike Ives and Alexandra Stevenson, "Hong Kong Police Face Criticism over Force Used at Protests," *The New York Times*, June 13, 2019.

76 Bilal Kuchay, "What You Should Know about India's 'Anti-Muslim' Citizenship Law," *Al Jazeera*, December 16, 2019.

77 Jeffrey Gettleman, Sameer Yasir, Suhasini Raj, and Hari Kumar, "How Delhi's Police Turned Against Muslims," *The New York Times*, March

the injustices that are amplified due to the passage of this amendment. In the past, this likely would not have been noted outside the South Asian region, but now, millions of people around the world can support the protests outside the country as well.

- Xinjiang "re-education" camps – In the past several months, the Chinese government has inflicted the forcible imprisonment of over one million ethnic Uyghur people in China.[78] The detention camps were labeled as "voluntary re-education camps" and attempted to hide the horrors that lie inside. The imprisoned people are subject to rape, starvation, forcible eating of food that is against their religion, etc.[79] There has been a social media blockade within the country, but stories and information about what has gone on inside the camps have been leaked. Awareness has been spread through social media, which has allowed for global attention to be directed toward China. While there has yet to be a substantial response, it is valuable to know there is a chance for people to know about these gross human rights violations so they can mobilize and hopefully stop them.

But while there can be many benefits to technology, there may be some downsides to the intense use of technology in protest movements and social change. In a TedTalk, Zeynep Tufekci, a writer, professor, and techno-sociologist, explains

---

12, 2020.

78   "Data Leak Reveals How China 'Brainwashes' Uighurs in Prison Camps," *BBC News*, November 24, 2019.

79   "China Uighurs: Detainees 'Free' after 'Graduating,' Official Says," *BBC News*, December 9, 2019.

that while technology has been wonderful in getting issues to receive global recognition, the movements planned online do not always pan out the way they were meant to. She believes in the past, when there wasn't such heavy dependency on technology, those involved in social movements built stronger connections, which then led to change that lasted longer and was more effective over time. Tufekci also believes the past used to present stronger leaders, while now it seems to be more about the quantity of people versus the connection between them. Since new issues and movements are constantly being promoted at a rapid pace, the passion for the movements tends to falter over time, which leads to lack of results and people becoming frustrated.[80]

One movement that comes to mind was the "Occupy Wall Street" protests in 2011. At the time, this movement received incredible attention, which allowed more people to understand the severity of the economic inequality issue within the United States.[81]

While it is considered a historic moment in modern history, I rarely remember hearing about it growing up, and I only learned about it almost a decade after it happened. We can point to many different factors—I was in the Midwest, I was only twelve when it happened, no one I knew worked on Wall Street or participated in the protest—but economic inequality

---

80   Zeynep Tufekci, "Online Social Change: Easy to Organize, Hard to Win," Filmed October 2014 in Rio de Janeiro, Brazil, TED video.

81   Michael Levitin, "The Triumph of Occupy Wall Street," *The Atlantic*, June 10, 2015.

affects the "bottom 99 percent" of American families.[82] Shouldn't 99 percent of us have heard about those fighting for an issue so relevant?

But regardless of how popularized the phrase became, this movement unfortunately suffered the same fate as many others. It lost its traction because not enough responses and changes were implemented in a timely fashion, so supporters got discouraged and stopped participating fully. There are many criticisms to consider as well—lack of clear goals, lack of minority representation, lack of measurable change. While the cause was noble, as they truly wanted a fair playing field that allowed upward mobility for all people, execution and consistency mainly impact the success of a movement.

If people will get tired of an issue eventually, is it even worth going through all that trouble in the first place? The answer will always be yes. Social movements will always have highs and lows; that's just the nature of a long battle. There's no way to completely avoid it, but we can't let the possibility of hitting a low dissuade us from fighting for our rights and better ways of life.

In my own life, even within my own household, I find myself arguing over and over for the things I care about. I have a yearly debate with my parents about my goals to work in global health; they want me to work in a hospital. I want to work on the ground, within the community. We consistently

---

82   Estelle Sommeiller and Mark Price, "The New Gilded Age: Income Inequality in the U.S. by State, Metropolitan Area, and County," Economic Policy Institute, July 19, 2018.

argue over my dedication to my dance teams; they will always be irritated by my unwillingness to let go of dance even when I'm stressed about school. To them, it's a waste of time if I'm not trying to be a professional dancer; to me, it's when I feel the most free and peaceful. I fight about the importance of addressing mental health issues in the South Asian community, while others tell me to not be so concerned about other people's "business."

Yet even though I constantly will be discouraged, or watch as the people around me eventually lose their passion for the things we both once cared about, I can't bring myself to follow suit. I know what's important to me, and I know that even if others don't agree or respond with the same intensity and conviction, the causes I'm advocating for still have the potential for change and growth.

Advocacy fatigue is a continuous challenge, but it doesn't negate the fact that social movements have more potential than ever before to create change on a much larger scale. If we can acknowledge these weaknesses, we can actively address them as we craft new movements to elicit a better global response. Strong leaders are still leading our movements today. They may spread their messages differently, but their integrity and dedication to their cause can be likened to the leaders of the past. Also, while there may not be smaller groups of intensely active members dedicated to the cause, these larger groups of people who support social movements still include many who are actively trying to make a difference. Technology is still a valuable tool and should be used to its full potential when attempting to connect people to each other and to a cause.

Yes, it's easy to blame technology, with all its downsides. Our current society faces many criticisms: we're a generation too dependent on our phones, we're connected online but disconnected in real life. But when we look at what it can do for us, the positives far outweigh the negatives. By teaching people how to effectively use the internet and social media to their advantage, there is no limit to how far a social movement can reach.

PART 2

WHAT IT TAKES

"The success of every woman should be the inspiration to another. We should raise each other up."

— SERENA WILLIAMS

CHAPTER 4

SUPPORT NETWORK

———

It was October 2017, the night before my huge biology midterm and first real college exam. The last thing I should've been doing was crouching in the corner of the second floor in the library, staring at my mom's shocked expression through FaceTime, but that's where I had ended up. I had just told my mom I had decided not to pursue medicine. I didn't want to be a doctor. I wanted to pursue public health full time instead. Rather than calmly ease her into the topic, I had awkwardly blurted it out because I couldn't handle the anxiety that accompanied the decision. The pause must have only lasted a few seconds, but it felt like hours were passing. I felt my heartbeat pick up speed as the magnitude of my words began to show on her face.

As I waited for her to respond, mixed emotions fought to take over me. A part of me felt free, but also guilty, ashamed, and anxious. This was the first time I'd ever made a decision for my own life, independent of anyone's opinions. I'd discovered a new field, one that resonated with my strengths, interests, and goals. It was like a fundamental truth had been uncovered. *I was meant to work in public health.* I tried to tell myself everything would be fine. My parents had always supported me and adored my hardworking nature and academic accomplishments. Surely they believed I would be successful doing anything, right?

"You've shattered my dreams."

It took a second to process this. Had I heard that right? A few more seconds went by in silence, but I struggled to keep track of them as I fought back tears. "Amma, I didn't mean-" I began, but my mom cut me off before I could finish.

"I'm so disappointed. I had so many dreams for you." My mom's cold, unfeeling tone was shocking. This was not the mother I was used to. The one I grew up with may have gotten angry with me, but even if there was fire behind her words, there was always a semblance of warmth. This, this was different. This was like she had shut off every emotion within herself, and to watch her do that was the most heartbreaking part.

I choked out a weak "I'm sorry," and she ended the call. I cried in that corner for who knows how long, and then sniffled my way back to my study table and picked up my biology book once again.

I don't blame my mom for her reaction; after all, both she and my dad had been so excited at the idea of having a doctor in the family. They were elated when they found out I had gotten into this direct program, even allowing me to move thousands of miles away for the opportunity. Even though they eventually came to terms with my new decision, it took months of phone calls that ended in passive-aggressive arguments. They are incredibly supportive of me now, but at that point in my life, it felt like everybody was against me.

Their reaction stemmed from their concern that I wouldn't be able to financially support myself, but at the time, they didn't know how to express that. Had I not had a support network that expanded past my immediate family, such as caring professors and friends who encouraged me to carve my own path, I'm not sure I would even be writing this book right now. I might've still been huddled back in that corner, crying over an exam on a subject I didn't want to study and stressed about a future I never wanted for myself.

We've all heard the phrase "it takes a village." But in modern society, it seems everyone is obsessed with doing everything independently. Many people perceive needing help as a sign of weakness, which prevents them from asking in the first place. But how valid is this concern in the grand scheme of things? Has greatness of any kind been achieved by one sole person?

Women everywhere are constantly barraged with barriers to advancement, and as much as we'd like to believe they can overcome them all independently, they can't. In the workplace, this can take the form of a lack of career development opportunities for women, or inaction from male managers on injustices faced by women in their offices.[83]

---

83   Rehab Mohammed, "What Is Barriers to Women Advancement?" Empower Women: Community Discussions, last modified December 24, 2016.

For women with children, lack of affordable childcare options can hinder their abilities to seek out economic opportunities that would improve their financial stability.[84] Sexism still runs rampant in many social interactions, whether it be among professional sports players, societal expectations of domestic responsibilities, or lack of confidence in women due to stereotypes. Women are incredibly capable, but they can only go so far by themselves; they need the support of others in multiple capacities to become truly empowered.

As I was interviewing various professionals about this topic, the conversation often naturally led to the competitive culture constantly attributed to the female population worldwide. The concept of "competing versus celebrating" is universal, and it is incredibly toxic. As women, we have an inherent connection between us, yet society has pitted us against each other, convincing us there is not enough space for all of us to flourish, for all of us to be valued.

In her book, *We Should All Be Feminists*, Chimamanda Ngozi Adichie states, "We raise girls to see each other as competitors not for jobs or accomplishments, which I think can be a good thing, but for the attention of men."[85] It has forced us to constantly compare ourselves to each other in every aspect of life, and encourages us to point out each other's flaws and failures to make ourselves feel better. Rather than

---

84   "The Barriers for Women in Career Advancement," UK Essays, Last modified December 1, 2018.

85   Chimamanda Ngozi Adichie, *We Should All Be Feminists* (New York: Vintage Books by Random House LLC, 2014). 32.

encouraging collaboration, we've chosen to isolate ourselves from each other, to be close but not too close.

While a few of us can probably climb our way to the top, are we truly okay with being alone up there without reaching back to help lift other women as well? When did we convince ourselves there wasn't enough space for all women to thrive? That success is a limited resource that must be carefully guarded by the "chosen few?" All these lies have clouded our judgment and continuously hold us down and apart because society knows when we band together, we're a force to be reckoned with.

But who should we ask to be part of our support networks?

FEMALE FRIENDS

When we're young, it seems like we're surrounded by a bunch of friends, but as we age, our groups tend to get smaller and smaller as life paths diverge. A child tends to have one or two close friends and a much wider range of playmates.[86] As a child, it's hard to understand what a friend really is besides someone to play with and accompany you.

In comparison, adults tend to have about nine close friends, but the relationships are much deeper than the ones maintained with their other friends or acquaintances.[87] These rela-

---

86   "Friends and Friendship: 10 Frequently Asked Questions," Raising Children: An Australian Parenting Website, Last modified November 17, 2017.

87   Joseph Carroll, "Americans Satisfied with Number of Friends, Closeness of Friendships," *Gallup,* March 5, 2004.

tionships often are cultivated through the sharing of struggles, interests, and a much wider variety of life experiences. As much as we cherish our friends for the fun memories we make, do we realize how much impact they can have on our journey as a woman throughout life? Female friends are essential to empowerment.

Research has found friendships can enhance women's health and mental wellbeing.[88] Regardless of age, the presence of other females supporting you is invaluable; they can serve as emotional support, offer career advice, influence your decisions, and provide honest opinions when you need it the most. In Ghana, a 2007 study discovered social institutions and friendships tended to be the sources of information and influence for the sexual and health needs of adolescents, after significant adults and parents.[89]

Our friends not only inform us but also hold great influence in decisions that positively or negatively impact our health, and our lives in general. By recognizing the power these relationships have, you will see how your own relationships have affected your life so far.

88   Geoffrey Grief and Tanya L. Sharpe, "The Friendships of Women: Are There Differences between African Americans and Whites?" *Journal of Human Behavior in the Social Environment* 20, no. 6 (August 2010): 791-807.

89   Akwasi Kumi-Kyereme et al., "Influence of Social Connectedness, Communication and Monitoring on Adolescent Sexual Activity in Ghana," *African Journal of Reproductive Health* 11, no. 1 (April 2007): 133-136.

Melissa Boguslawski, a professor at Nova Southeastern University, could not imagine getting to where she is now without the support of her core group of female friends. These women don't just blindly support her in everything she does. Rather than stay silent to avoid conflict, they voice their honest opinions to help her grow, even if they're not opinions that she wants to hear.

"You can't be afraid to be honest or challenge people," Boguslawski revealed to me, "If you know what the other person is capable of, and they're not performing to their highest potential, you need to push them when necessary." She stressed the importance of accountability within friendships, and how women need to look out for each other.

So how do you become this type of friend for the women in your life? First, be observant. If a friend looks burnt out, it's an opportunity to remind her to take time for self-care and to reset. If your friend keeps talking about a long-term goal yet never makes an effort to start pursuing it, ask, "What's going on? Is there anything I can help you with? What's making it difficult for you to get this done?"

At times, it's necessary to peel back the layers. Women carry a lot with them at all times (and I'm not talking about our tendency to over-stuff our purses). There are so many layers to our daily struggles that often it is difficult to identify the roots of our issues ourselves. However, having strong female friends around us makes it easier to identify our barriers to success and create strategies to overcome them. Working together to come up with solutions often can be better than attempting to solve our issues on our own.

Young women around the world have discovered the importance of female friendships, and they've actively taken steps to create spaces for these relationships to form. The GenZ Girl Gang, founded by Deja Foxx, is a community open to anyone of any age or gender identity/expression that centers "GenZ women and femmes" as the content creators and leaders. As explained by Foxx on the platform's Instagram, it aims to "redefine sisterhood" through three means: bridging generational gaps, creating and sharing opportunities, and learning from and teaching one another. By community sourcing its content, its members are flipping the normal social media script and choosing a bottom-up method of disseminating information.[90]

Thousands have flocked to this community, and the organization provides the opportunity for lesser-known organizations and advocates to reach a larger audience through its platform. These changemakers are not only friends but also support each other in their various endeavors and social causes. They network with each other, amplify events through social media, and provide space to express their struggles and realizations. As a collective, the members exemplify the power of women supporting each other at any age.

As I was researching the GenZ Girl Gang, I stumbled upon the profile of its associate director, Pranjal Jain. Her thoughtful posts on South Asian culture, feminism, and representation intrigued me, and I immediately reached out to ask her about her experience with the group.

90   Deja Foxx, "GenZ Girl Gang," Instagram.

As soon as our call started, I could tell Pranjal was the type of girl who got things done. Her matter-of-fact nature and confident way of answering my questions offered a refreshing change of pace for me as an interviewer. Pranjal never hesitated too long to answer, and her passion for her work clearly shone through in our conversation.

When I asked about how the GenZ Girl Gang has affected her life, Pranjal said she found her "tribe" within this group. She believes in the strength of "radical sisterhood," which she describes as "being there for your sisters no matter what, showing up for them, believing in them, and going the extra mile for them." Pranjal detailed how she found power in several key things: in creating space for all kinds of women, in believing in people when they may not believe in themselves, and in giving them chances. "After all," she continued earnestly, "there's no reason [we all] can't be successful."

Pranjal has found a strong community, drawing inspiration from her colleagues and the many others they highlight on their platform. In her eyes, realizing the power and potential women have, along with creating community, are the key factors of female empowerment.

MALE ALLIES

While it may not be focused on enough in the media, having men on our side is vital to the movement toward equality. The United Nations Statistics Division has found that throughout the world, men hold many of the decision-making positions that affect women in all areas, whether in the health field, access to education, judiciary processes, or economic resource disbursement.[91]

If we don't include men in the effort toward gender equality, progress will be slow-moving, if it even goes very far at all. Back in 2014, UN Goodwill Ambassador Emma Watson spoke at the launch of the HeForShe campaign in New York. In her passionate speech for gender equality, she posed a profound question to the audience: "How can we effect change in the world when only half of it is invited or feels welcome to participate in the conversation?"[92]

Although it may not feel like it, many men do support women's rights and equality. Many of the female role models we see in society today often had some type of male support, whether through friendship, the support of a partner, or a mentor in the workforce. In fact, Jiji John, the chief of staff to the Managed Care & Customer Operations team at Genentech, strongly advocates for male allies because of her past experiences.

At the beginning of her career, she had been told putting her head down and working hard would get her the recognition she had earned. However, she quickly realized those who don't have advocates, let alone those who don't advocate for themselves, often are overlooked in the professional world.

91   United Nations Statistics Division, "Chapter 5: The Power and Decision-Making," *The World's Women 2015*, (2015), 119-138.

92   United Nations, "Emma Watson at the HeForShe Campaign 2014 – Official UN Video," September 22, 2014, video, 13:15.

Fortunately, Dennis, a male colleague, opened the door to opportunity by advocating for her to take a sales role for the company's largest U.S. client. Before this experience, she had never worked in sales before, so she didn't believe she was qualified for the position. Yet Dennis persisted, saying her capability, not her experience, was necessary for the role; the skills could be taught on the job. With his encouragement, she took the sales roles, which helped launch her career in ways she could never have imagined.

"You can't just have women helping women," Jiji says. "You need men too. You need people in the majority to say, 'There is a need and value in bringing different perspectives to the table.'"

Many men throughout the world are committed to fighting for gender equality alongside women, whether by directing women to proper resources, taking part in conversations about gender inequality, calling out misogynistic behavior such as inappropriate comments, or making sure their female colleagues are getting their proper space to speak and deserved credit where it's due.

HeForShe, according to its mission statement, is a "global solidarity movement that invites men and people of all genders to create a bold, visible, and united force for gender equality."[93] It seeks to encourage these populations to become agents of change by taking active stances against negative stereotypes and behaviors. Rather than stay on the sidelines to the injustices facing women, the men involved in this

93   United Nations, "HeforShe," UN Women, accessed June 8, 2020.

campaign are working with women and each other to raise families, build businesses, and give back to their communities. Millions of people have committed to the cause, and it has inspired people across the world to work within their own communities to promote change.

In Jordan, Laith Abu-Taleb works on redefining masculinity throughout the country by addressing the negative stereotypes about women and about what it takes to "be a man." He alone has mobilized over 22,000 commitments to HeForShe and continues to encourage other men to understand social equality is not just a women's issue but a men's issue as well. In his Equality Story on HeForShe's website, he states, "Now is the time to stand together and make our voices heard, because each of our voices is important enough to make a difference."[94]

Saket Mani, an Indian HeForShe supporter, leads advocacy workshops in rural India to positively shift the gender norms that traditionally have been disempowering for women. The workshops promote the creation of youth advocacy networks and encourage people to take up initiatives at a community level to, as he states, "instill a sense of 'belongingness." This method allows people to freely support the cause and implies a sense of personal agency in the battle against negative stereotypes.[95]

94 UN Women, "HeforShe Equality Story: Redefining Masculinity in Jordan," September 27, 2016. Video, 2:44.

95 UN Women, "HeforShe Equality Story: Cycling for Gender Equality in Rural India," September 27, 2016. Video, 2:11.

Plan International, a Canadian organization dedicated to the spread of children's rights, uses gender equality as a foundation to remove the barriers that keep children, especially young girls, from reaching their potential. They've launched a program called Champions of Change, which seeks to assist young boys in acknowledging their privileges and advantages and see the opportunities they have to eliminate sexism from their lives. They learn responsibility regarding sexuality, how being non-violent is essential in personal relationships, and how to encourage solidarity and commitment to gender equality throughout their lives.[96]

Even changing their family and home dynamic will spark change. According to the United Nations Population Fund, for opposite-sex couples, "Promoting programmes to enable women and men to reconcile their work and family responsibilities" will help distribute domestic tasks between partners, creating a more equal share of responsibility between the couple rather than allowing typical gender norms to place the majority on the woman.[97]

Men can contribute to the female empowerment movement in so many ways. If we want to gain more male support, we must emphasize gender equality doesn't mean life will become worse for men. Rather, it's about creating a fair world for all people to live in. By working together, we can elevate the quality of life for entire nations.

---

96 Plan International Canada Inc., "Plan International: What We Do," last modified 2019.

97 United Nations Funds for Public Activities, "Issue 7: Women Empowerment," (Cairo, UNFPA, 1994).

FAMILY

Family doesn't have to be limited to blood relations, but your family does tend to hold one of the strongest influences over your life, regardless of your age. In fact, social relationships, especially those found within close families, have been shown to decrease the likelihood of many negative health consequences, such as the onset of chronic disease, mental illness, disability, and even death.[98] Those who receive support from their family may feel a greater sense of self-esteem and self-worth, which can act as a psychological resource that encourages positive disposition, optimism, and overall better mental health.[99] Positive relationships can serve as a protective factor to stress, which will improve a person's overall health.

But not just the affect-related influences are important; the behavioral influences of family are also vital to a person's health. Family members often regulate each other's behavior and can potentially provide information and encouragement to behave in healthier ways or to utilize health care resources more effectively.[100]

---

98   Unite for Sight, "Module 1: Family Dynamics and Health," Unite for Sight, last modified 2020.

99   Patricia A. Thomas, Hiu Liu, and Debra Umberson, "Family Relationships and Well-Being," *Innovation in Aging* 1, no. 3 (November 2017): 1-11.

100 Corinne Reczek et al., "Diet and Exercise in Parenthood: A Social Control Perspective," Reczek, Corinne et al. "Diet and Exercise in Parenthood: A Social Control Perspective." *Journal of Marriage and the Family* 76, no. 5 (2014): 1047-1062.

However, just as they can be a positive influence in someone's life, families can, unfortunately, negatively impact health as well. If someone grows up in an unsupported, violent, or neglectful home, it can be associated with their poor physical health and development.[101] If such relationships promote stress, it can lead to health-compromising behaviors, such as unhealthy coping mechanisms like alcohol or drug abuse.[102]

For women around the world, family is often at the center of their lives—they're not only typically the main caretakers, but also often have to be subject to the decisions and whims of other family members who have power over them, whether due to cultural/gender norms or other negative circumstances. Family power dynamics and gender roles can negatively impact a woman's health and her ability to seek health care.

Many cultures throughout the world require a woman to seek permission from other family members, such as a husband, father, or mother-in-law, to access health services. For example, in a survey conducted about reproductive health, women in Malawi (and other developing countries) have little power regarding decisions about using resources, and must seek their husband's approval before incurring health care costs.[103] A study on gender taboos in Afghanistan found men continued to prevent women from receiving care from

101 Linda K. George, "The Health-Promoting Effects of Social Bonds," Duke University, 2016.

102 Thomas, Liu, and Umberson, "Family Relationships and Well-Being."

103 "REACH: Challenging Barriers to Health Care," Department for International Development, January 1, 2005.

male medical staff in hospitals, even in life-threatening conditions.[104] Another survey stated 12 percent of Afghan women didn't give birth in a health care structure because their husbands didn't allow it.[105]

Cultural associations and norms regarding health care are often perpetuated by family members as well. For example, a common attitude in many cultures is that medical treatment is only for serious or life-threatening illnesses or injuries; minor illnesses are often not treated until they produce visible signs or become unbearably painful. In Turkey, a study found about 30 percent of all pregnancy-related deaths were due to delayed health seeking by the family, as Turkish people often don't seek treatment unless signs become visible.[106] Looking at these results, it's clear to see how dangerous these limitations can be for any person, especially women.

Family members often don't have bad intentions. They are simply following generations of attitudes toward health care and gender norms, or are simply not well-informed or educated about the necessity or value of certain resources.[107] In

---

104   Ron Synovitz, "Afghanistan: Gender Taboos Keep Women from Seeking Medical Care," Radio Free Europe, March 3, 2004, accessed June 8, 2020.

105   IbnSina and ICRH, "KAP Survey regarding reproductive health," October 2002, accessed June 8, 2020.

106   Pinar Ay et al., "The Influence of Gender Roles on Health Seeking Behaviour during Pregnancy in Turkey," *The European Journal of Contraception and Reproductive Health Care* 14, no. 4 (August 2009): 290-300.

107   Shaheen Sheikh and A. Furnham, "A Cross-Cultural Study of Mental Health Beliefs and Attitudes toward Seeking Professional Help," *Soc Psychiatry Psychiatric Epidemiology* 35, no. 1 (2000): 326-334.

many communities, a cost is associated with health services, whether it be monetary, time, etc. Also, there can be negative views on medical professionals and services. Some may believe they are promoting negatively viewed behaviors, such as the provision of sexual education and/or contraception to young men and women, even though their culture forbids pre-marital sex.[108] Others may simply believe medical professionals don't have the best intentions, or don't respect the culture and traditions of the community.[109]

Even non-medical decisions, such as allowing girls to be educated, often reflect an adopted attitude from the general community rather than the individual family. In many countries, it's simply a fact of life that girls are only meant to reach a minimal level of education, if they're even allowed to pursue one at all. The idea that girls must be primed to be wives/mothers/caretakers negatively impacts their chances for education. Ziauddin Yousafzai, Malala Youfaszai's father, noticed many of his female friends and cousins "disappeared" as he aged, often married off or kept at home to perform domestic tasks.

He recognized this was merely a cultural norm. He had lived in a patriarchal community within Pakistan, and any

---

108 Robab Latifnejad Roudsari et al., "Socio-Cultural Challenges to Sexual Health Education for Female Adolescents in Iran," *Iranian Journal of Reproductive Medicine* 11, no. 2 (2013): 101-10.

109 Joseph Maaminu Kyilleh, Philip Teg-Nefaah Tabong, and Benson Boinkum Konlaan, "Adolescents' Reproductive Health Knowledge, Choices and Factors Affecting Reproductive Health Choices: A Qualitative Study in the West Gonja District in Northern Region, Ghana," *BMC International Health and Human Rights* 18,no. 6 (2018).

challenge to the system would be met with not just disdain but active backlash from others within his community. But in his mind, it wasn't enough to be treated well just because he was a man; there had to be a way to promote gender equality, and he realized it had to start with the families that made up the communities.[110]

What do families need to do, then? Well, it depends on the woman and the family itself. In some cases, a shift in cultural attitudes to improve the health outcomes of a community may be necessary. In others, families may need to be more proactive and be willing to step up and offer more help.

For example, one of the most underappreciated determinants of overall health and well-being is affordable access to childcare. In a 2018 survey conducted for the Center for American Progress, mothers were 40 percent more likely than fathers to report feeling the negative effects of child care issues on their careers.[111] If a mother doesn't have access to affordable childcare, they are limited in the economic opportunities they can pursue, which means they also may be unable to provide the best resources for their families. In the United States alone, the cost of lost earnings, productivity, and revenue due to the childcare crisis comes close to an estimated $57 billion each year.[112]

---

110   Aoife Barry, "'I Tell People: Girls and Women in Patriarchal Societies, They Die as if They Were Never Born,'" *The* Journal.ie, November 19, 2018.

111   John Halpin, Karl Agne, and Margie Omero, "Affordable Child Care and Early Learning for All Families," Center for American Progress, 2018.

112   Sandra Bishop-Josef et al., "Want to Grow the Economy? Fix the Child Care Crisis," Ready Nation, Council for A Strong America, January 2019.

Having families that support one another by taking care of children allows women to pursue financial opportunities they perhaps couldn't take advantage of before. Access to economic opportunities increases the household income, which, in turn, allows women to afford more health care resources, opportunities for higher education, and other beneficial goods and services to improve their overall well-being and the quality of life for others.

Ziauddin Yousafzai started by refusing to hold his wife to the patriarchal restrictions society demanded. He treated his daughter and sons equally. He became a teacher and opened a school for both boys and girls and became an activist for gender equality.[113] His daughter, Malala, later became one of the most recognizable advocates of girls' education of all time.

In an interview with the Journal.ie, he explained how creating change requires you to defeat your old self and refuse to stay in the comfort zone of what society expects.[114] For families, this can be invaluable advice when it comes to choosing to be open to shifting a perspective on women's rights to health and education. But creating this shift sometimes requires outside assistance.

When it comes to changing preconceived notions, Angeline Makore is one changemaker who has understood the necessity of family involvement for empowering young girls. Zimbabwe has one of the highest rates of child marriage; about one in three girls will be married off before they are

113   Aoife Barry, "I tell people..."
114   Ibid.

eighteen.[115] Makore herself was in danger of being married off at fourteen, after she discovered her brother-in-law was planning to make her his second wife. Intrigued by her story, I reached out and asked her to tell me about herself. Graciously, Angeline illustrated exactly what this tumultuous time was like.

While she had before been comfortable with her sister and brother-in-law, she noticed an increasingly alarming change in his behavior months before the discussion of her marriage. Seemingly out of nowhere, he began showering Angeline with superfluous compliments, bodily praises, and many gifts, even going so far to "jokingly" introduce her as his "young wife" to other relatives and church members.

"It became weird to me to the extent that I became scared of the motives," she enlightened me through a descriptive email. However, due to her youth, she attempted to dismiss the behavior, as, according to Angeline, culturally the brother-in-law takes care of his wife's relatives. But at one point, she couldn't deny that there was an underlying motive behind his "generosity."

"As time went on, I started seeing an increase in suggestive gestures. For example, him telling my mother that I could be his second wife." I couldn't believe it when she told me that; even with such direct signs, her mother and sister never

115   Zimbabwe National Statistics Agency, "Zimbabwe Demographic and Health Survey 2015: Final Report," (Rockville, Maryland, U.S.A.: Zimbabwe National Statistics Agency (ZIMSTAT) and ICF International), November 2016.

suspected it was serious. But Angeline saw the red flags, especially when it escalated and he wanted to force her to convert to his "apostolic sect faith" in which having many wives was the norm during that time.

"One thing that made me return to my parents' house and never return to my sister's was when my sister's husband began to send his brothers and older sister to convince me to marry him." After providing such undeniable evidence of his intentions, Angeline realized she could not fall for such antics and managed to avoid being married off to him.

This experience ignited her resolve to prevent more young girls from suffering such a fate. She founded Spark R.E.A.D., which reflects her desire to "Spark Resilience, Empowerment, Activism, and the Development of girls."[116] She's saved many victims of child marriage and sexual abuse and seeks to educate others on reproductive, maternal, newborn, child, and adolescent health issues. Above all, she said she aims to "holistically empower girls and women to be the main authors of their life journey."

"One fundamental thing about early forced child marriage is its diversity in cornering tactics," she said. "In my situation, as young as I was, tricks were played on me. I did not fall for it, but not every girl child out there has the autonomy or the power to say NO or deny being forced into an early marriage. I narrowly escaped a child marriage and am forever grateful I had the courage to read between bad and good intentions."

116 "Celebrating Change-Makers: Angeline, Putting Girls at the Centre of Change in Zimbabwe," Girls Not Brides, June 7, 2017.

Makore understands girls are often taken out of school and married off due to the cultural norms, and families in the community hesitate to step up, as they are reluctant to get involved in another family's affairs. But change can only begin when discussion does.

One way Makore promotes alternative paths for young women is by running workshops for parents and families, which teach them about the dangers of child marriage and show them the other paths their daughters can take. These workshops educate young boys on how to be advocates for change as well.

"At Spark R.E.A.D, we practice a mantra which we call 'NO to leaving anyone behind,'" she said. "Our programs focus more on the girls and women; however, we noticed that these girls/women are not left in a vacuum. This means they have older women, parents, fathers, teachers, brothers, etc., who surround them. Therefore, if we seldom include these people, then our messaging will not be effective enough."

To illustrate this concept, she offered an example involving busting menstruation taboos. "We involve parents and boys because [when] they are equipped with [the] correct information, they are able to dismantle the taboos through parent-to-parent or peer-to-peer [communication]. In addition, when we put inclusiveness at the forefront of our programs, we usually see quick results because there is a diverse [set] of contributions with a common goal, whereby teachers, parents, and community duty bearers such as chiefs [work] together to combat early forced child marriages."

By involving the families at various levels and providing opportunities for them to be educated, she gives them the chance to see why they should be making different decisions, rather than simply telling them their way of life is wrong. In a similar manner, we should also encourage education and discussion among families so they may find ways to support the young women around them, whether through challenging cultural norms or by giving young women the freedom to explore various career paths.

MENTORS AND SPONSORS

Mentors are vital for creating a strong support network for young women. While people may consider a mentor an additional resource, a quality mentor can benefit a mentee in innumerable ways, such as improving self-confidence, communication skills, and leadership capabilities.[117]

In 2017, a study on mentor and role model influence on female university leaders found 87.5 percent of participants lacked a primary career mentor and/or role model.[118] Many of the participants attributed this to the fact that they did not initially have aspirations for higher positions within the university at the beginning of their career.

---

117 "The Importance of Mentors for Girls and Young Women," Girls Empowerment Network, February 4, 2015.

118 Lilian H. Hill and Celeste A. Wheat, "The Influence of Mentorship and Role Models on University Women Leaders' Career Paths to University Presidency," *The Qualitative Report* 22, no. 8 (2008): 2090-2111.

However, how many women are encouraged to the same degree as men to aspire to these types of positions in the first place? If most high-level positions are taken up by men, and people tend to identify best with younger workers who are the same sex, then a huge disparity exists between the number of mentors available for women and the number of women who need a mentor.

Everyone who has achieved great success can attribute part of it to having great mentors throughout their journey. In an interview with WCVB-TV 5 News, CityLine, Oprah Winfrey talked about how mentors are the key to any type of achievement. "I don't think anybody makes it in the world without some form of mentorship," she stated. "Nobody makes it alone. Nobody has made it alone."[119]

Considering one of the most objectively successful and recognizable women on the planet actively emphasizes the impact of a mentor, it's safe to say mentorship is a vital component to any woman's success, in whatever she endeavors to accomplish.

When Pranjal Jain, founder of Global Girlhood, joined her local Girl Scouts chapter as a child, she didn't realize she would find a lifelong mentor in her troop leader, Chris. Pranjal is like any other student; she works hard, plays hard, and, most importantly, wants to leave an impact in the world. But she revealed that she owed her passion for advocacy to Chris. "She pushed me to realize the power of my voice," she

---

119   Oprah Winfrey, interview by WCVB-TV 5 News CityLine, Boston, U.S.A., January 13, 2002.

responded when interviewed. "She really listens to me, and finding that in an older person can be hard sometimes. She also lets me explore and learn for myself, and never pushes her ideals and opinions on me."

Mentors can help address potential career/life concerns and convey strategies to overcome these struggles. They may provide suggestions on how to expand one's network, on how to create a vision for a career, and on potential areas for growth, both personally and professionally.

Most of the time, their insight can help increase a mentee's visibility within an organization and help advance their careers with the mentor's years of experience to refer to. "I think of [Chris] as the translator between my ideas and passions to the community," Pranjal said thoughtfully. "Her wisdom and experiences transcend onto me, but when I have an idea or opinion, she never just says 'Pranjal, you're wrong.'"

They've come to value a give-and-take relationship, in which both people can learn from each other and their respective experiences. For Pranjal, Chris represented something greater than just an ally. Chris taught her the power of believing in yourself and believing your dreams are attainable. Especially for Pranjal, who, growing up, "never saw people who looked like [her], had experiences as [her], who did the work that [she] wanted to do," her mentor gave her the confidence to believe she could achieve whatever she wanted.

But mentors are not the only important person for a woman attempting to achieve new heights; sponsors are equally important as well. While mentors may provide career advice and guidance, sponsors serve as advocates. Rather than a mentee, they are looking for a protégé—someone they can help open doors for and recommend for various higher-level positions.

For women, a sponsor is critical. Without someone who is actively willing to advocate for their achievements and capabilities, it is a lot more difficult for women to be considered for certain opportunities over their male counterparts.

According to Stanford SLAC's Division of Diversity and Inclusion, sponsors hold a different set of advantages when compared to a mentor. Rather than spend most of their time guiding, they are focused on actively using their established connections to elevate the success of their protégé. They're usually a senior-level member invested in the career success of the protégé and wish to help drive his/her career vision. Sponsors often use their own platforms to increase one's visibility, and they actively exhibit model behavior and involve their protégés in experiences that are conducive to their advancement.[120]

Both mentors and sponsors are necessary in different regards, as mentors advise you and help you find your path, while sponsors can help open the right doors and even help you get your foot in. Yet getting such valuable resources can be incredibly difficult for women. One of the main deterrents for mentoring women is the fact that, as mentioned before, men hold most of the roles in power and decision-making

---

120 Maryann Baumgarten, "The Key Role of Sponsorship," SLAC National Accelerator Laboratory, Stanford University, accessed June 8, 2020.

across the world. A stigma is associated with male-female mentorship/sponsorship; many people believe the diminishing stereotype that "it is almost impossible to have strong, intense relationships limited to non-sexual aspects."[121]

This negative connotation associated with opposite-gender mentor and mentee pairings can cause leaders to hesitate to form them, as they don't wish to have this stigma associated with themselves or their organization. But as we saw in Jiji John's experience, this stereotype is merely blocking women from success, and such baseless stereotypes need to be actively addressed to keep them from restricting the potential of women.

Women should have the freedom to accomplish their goals, not just for themselves but because they will inspire future generations as well. Female mentors are especially important to other women. Dr. Lucia Gilbert of Santa Clara University, through an interview with Girls Empowerment Network, explained how "not only do female students need mentors, they particularly need female mentors who can model the greater diversity in women's lives today."[122]

According to her research, female students over male students rated a same-sex mentor's lifestyle and values as highly important when it came to their own professional

121   Silvia Ines Monserrat et al., "Mentoring Experiences of Successful Women across the Americas," *Gender in Management: An International Journal* 24, no. 6 (2009): 455-476

122   "The Importance of Mentors for Girls and Young Women," Girls Empowerment Network, February 4, 2015.

development. Dr. Gilbert also stresses female students who have female mentors may provide an "antidote" to the common female socialization to please and defer to me. It even benefits both sides; both parties can learn through this relationship how to mobilize the strengths, energies, and resources of each individual.[123]

Remember when my mom told me I had shattered her dreams? I learned a valuable lesson from that experience. I may have shattered my mom's dreams by pursuing a different path, but I was able to pick up those pieces and forge an even greater dream for myself. Once I'd created my new dream, my support network saw just how bright my future could be. But if my family had never challenged me, if I'd never had people question my motives, my passions, my drive, I might have never found the conviction and determination I have now. I might have never learned to hold my ground, to stand strong in what I believed in, to use my voice and fight for the future I wanted.

Women need staunch supporters and people who will offer different perspectives. It's how we grow, how we evolve, and how we discover new paths and ideas and become the people we want to be. Most importantly, we need people to support and guide us rather than deny us the chance to make mistakes or take risks.

With so many different levels that make up a support network, it can be difficult to know where to begin. However, networks like this are built one person at a time, so rather

---

123 Ibid.

than spend time stressing over what will be the most effective relationship to cultivate, start with whichever one makes the most sense with your current situation. Support networks are important; they are not only related to career success but also to improved health outcomes for women and families, increased access to economic opportunities, social benefits, and positive mental health. If every young woman had the strength of a full-bodied support network behind her, she would have the resources to not only succeed but also to fail, with the comfort of knowing she has people on her team who are willing to help her get back on track.

CHAPTER 5

AUTHENTICITY

———

Shrill. Aggressive. No-nonsense. Bossy. Do these words come to mind when you think of female leaders?

There appears to be a specific formula women need to follow. We must act a certain way in order to succeed. We need to hide any part of ourselves that makes us seem "feminine," whether it be our physical self, our thoughts, our emotions, or our ways of speaking and being. Otherwise, we'll get squashed underneath everyone else fighting for the same thing. So why, now, is there a sudden call for authenticity among women in leadership?

Besides the fact that it benefits your personal relationships, authenticity is correlated to leadership potential, and studies show it can potentially accelerate women's impact within organizations. In a Deloitte survey, half the professionals indicated they believed leaders should be more authentic to help the organization further succeed. It also increases your sense of happiness and fulfillment, in your work and your life outside of it, too.[124]

All of this begs the question: what is authenticity? Authenticity, as defined by the Stanford Encyclopedia of Philosophy, is acting in accordance with desires, motives, ideals, or beliefs that are not only yours, as opposed to someone else's, but that also express who you really are.[125]

It seems easy to be authentic; after all, we're all born an individual, and no one else possesses the same external and internal qualities as another. Still, rather than embracing who we are, our society has placed an impossible paradox of standards on women. Studies have shown that if women embrace "feminine" qualities such as being kind, they're seen as less competent, but if they exhibit more "masculine" qualities such as self-confidence, they are often liked less and are not considered for leadership opportunities.[126] With such a fine line to balance, it's no surprise so many women feel the need to modify their behavior to accomplish their goals and gain the respect of their colleagues.

124 Janet Foutty, Terri Cooper, and Shelley Zalis, "Redefining Leadership: The Inclusion Imperative," Deloitte, June 2018, accessed June 8, 2020.

125 Somogy Varga and Charles Guignon, "Authenticity," The Stanford Encyclopedia of Philosophy, ed. Edward N. Zalta, Spring 2020, accessed June 8, 2020.

126 Jasmien Khattab, "Why It's Harder for Women to Be Seen as Authentic, Effective Leaders," Rotterdam School of Management, Erasmus University, June 27, 2017.

This tendency is known as the "covering" phenomenon. This concept explains that many women tend to have trouble expressing their true selves without risking social penalty in the workplace and other professional environments. They often do things like change their mannerisms or attire.[127] They may avoid "feminine" behaviors or remain silent when they encounter sexist jokes. Women often fear losing their jobs or being ostracized from work culture if they don't change or—even more unforgivable—commit the cardinal sin of pointing out the negative stereotypes and diminishing behaviors of others in their environment.

As much as I wish I could say I've never been this woman, I'm as guilty as the next person. I used to feel the need to appear effortlessly flawless so people would like me. I masked every negative emotion with a smile, stayed silent as people mistreated me, and pretended all the work I was doing "wasn't that hard." Whenever someone asked how I was doing, I automatically brightened and said, "I'm good! How about you?" rather than admit I was tired, stressed, or even on the brink of tears. Deflection was my signature because if I was busy asking other people about their lives and feelings, it often led to them forgetting to push me to share mine.

Yet as I got older, the only thing that resulted from all this effort was this constant feeling of exhaustion. No amount of external validation was enough. I looked at everyone else's lives from the outside: how did they seem like they had it all together? It seemed like every person was cultivating an

127   "Authenticity," The Women's Foundation, June 12, 2018.

image of perfection without any work at all. Why was my life the only one that was imperfect? But that's where I was wrong.

No one's life is as perfect as we make it out to be. In fact, most of the time, they're about as confused and stressed as you are. Unfortunately, we've cultivated a culture in which we all try to create the illusion that everything's going great, that we're never struggling. We often are left wondering who would want to see who we really are? Why would we show our lows when we could only show our highs? Why not pretend to be the person we want everyone to think we are, because isn't that how we get closer to actually becoming that person?

But having an authentic voice allows you a different power: it prompts stronger connections with others. People don't resonate with an untouchable image of perfection; people form stronger connections over shared experiences. In general, when people sense an alignment with your words and your actions, it invokes a sense of dependability. While it may be undervalued in some places, there is power in staying true to your values, which set you apart from others.

Sally Helgesen has been a women's leadership expert for over thirty years and has researched the various key elements of strong female leaders and inclusive work cultures. Traveling across the world, she's reached an innumerable amount of people with her insights on the barriers to women's success, citing both their self-made blocks and the obstacles society places in front of them.

When I asked for her take on authenticity, she offered a multi-leveled approach. "The reason authenticity is important in a leader is because people want a leader whose words they can trust, whose actions align with their words. How much do your actions reflect what you say is important to you?" From what she's learned, it's not about the statements we make but about the evidence of the intentions we set out. "Women can benefit from being a little more willing to take risks in what people think of them," she said thoughtfully. Rather than be concerned about what others think of us, we need to strive for consistency.

Helgesen also warned me about the dangers of simply encouraging young women to be authentic. "What is most effective is an authenticity that is real and has a degree of discipline. Having an awareness of your strengths and the challenges you may face is essential." She has witnessed people refuse to improve upon their weaknesses or stay stagnant in their mindsets because they claim authenticity as a justification. Her emphasis on self-awareness followed up by action separates those who use authenticity as an excuse from those who can authentically lead successfully.

To be an authentic leader, it's important to recognize there is no "one type" of successful leader. There are many different types of leaders, and different groups of people will flock toward them. The path to successful leadership begins with figuring out what kind of leader you want to be, then finding a flock with shared sensibilities.

For example, take two different young female changemakers who have made international headlines: Malala Yousafzai and Nadya Okamoto. Malala is about as different from your stereotypical female leader as you can get. She is calm, more reserved, and tends to be soft-spoken, even when her message is so powerful. When talking about the past, she is far from angry; she is gracious and has been forgiving toward the men who attacked her. Malala gently wields her strength with humility. For certain groups of people, she's a breath of fresh air and an active contrast to the stereotype of "the angry feminist."

Nadya, on the other hand, has approached her movement with full force. She is a self-proclaimed "hustler" and is far more active when discussing her opinions and demonstrating her emotions and thoughts on social media. She unabashedly calls out various instances of inequality and the people who perpetuate it. She falls into the typical heuristic for a female changemaker: a force of nature concealed within a woman's body. Due to this, she may be considered more "vibrant" or "interesting" to certain populations.

Neither approach is wrong; they're just different. Both have achieved marvelous things in a short time. Malala has won a Nobel Peace Prize for her advocacy for girls' education. And by pressuring many U.S. states to abolish antiquated "luxury good" taxes on feminine hygiene products, Nadya has helped make those products more accessible to women.

Their respective successes and followings demonstrate you can still accomplish your goals by doing them your way, and that there is no need to conform to societal expectations of what an effective leader looks like.

You don't always have to reinvent the wheel—being authentic doesn't mean you have to come up with a new idea.

Authenticity is doing things in a manner that corresponds with who you are and who you are growing to be. A clear example of this is the journey of Suhani Jalota, a young Indian woman who founded the Myna Mahila Foundation when she was studying at Duke University in 2015.

Like Nadya, Suhani's organization seeks to make feminine hygiene products accessible to women in need. However, her specific message with the Myna Mahila Foundation has struck a chord with an array of supporters, including Prince Harry and Meghan Markle. The organization's name—Myna Mahila—derives from the famously talkative "myna" bird and the word "mahila," which means "woman." Suhani wishes to not only open conversation about a taboo subject but also wants to open doors for the women of the Mumbai slums so they can empower themselves and live stable, financially independent lives.[128]

I decided to call Suhani to learn about her mission. And from the moment she said hello, I could feel the quiet confidence emanating from her. I'd heard glowing things about Suhani from many people, so I was slightly intimidated to speak with her. But talking with her became one of the highlights of my research period, as she was not only incredibly open with her story but also very intentional and thoughtful in her answers.

"Suhani," I asked, "how did you realize you wanted to start Myna Mahila at such a young age? It's hard enough to talk about a taboo subject when you're older, but how did you know this is what you were meant to do?"

---

128 Myna Mahila Foundation, accessed June 8, 2020.

But Suhani merely chuckled and said when she had started working in Mumbai's Govandi slums at fourteen years old, she didn't realize she was starting an organization. "I had no clear sense of what my values were, and I was still trying to explore them." She took each lesson one at a time, noting what things really frustrated her and what she admired. "I see so many mistakes in what I've done, and I'm wrong in so many ways. But rather than stay still, I look to others making similar mistakes and watch them overcome them. I've started observing others and learning from them."

To Suhani, any organization is a direct manifestation of the values of its founder. "My weaknesses and strengths are reflected in Myna," she confided, "and I have to improve as a person to improve Myna." When I asked how she remains authentic in her work, she said she has insisted the organization uphold core values. For example, she hadn't realized how important the traits of integrity and honesty would be in Myna. "No one can ever lie about anything at Myna—dishonesty isn't ever accepted. We are willing to spend that extra time to set a good norm in our organization."

While some people may believe in cutting corners to reach an end goal, Suhani has chosen to uphold sincerity as one of the key aspects of Myna Mahila's work. "Whatever we do, we have to give it our all. Putting in the hard work, being genuine about dedicating ourselves and our time, speaking with others about meeting our goals—this authenticity to our mission is what allows us to grow and be successful."

In Suhani's journey as a changemaker, she's realized being authentic to who she is and what she believes in separates

Myna Mahila from any other organization. Her dedication to setting goals and standards that are genuine to its mission is one of the main reasons she's come so far and will continue to go even further.

One of the most uncomfortable aspects of authenticity is that it cannot be accomplished without vulnerability. Authenticity inevitably will be met with opposition, but your message becomes more powerful when you show the world you will stay true to who you are, regardless of the social consequences. Poet Rupi Kaur has used her vulnerability to create a revolution through her writing. While she may not be initially thought of as a female changemaker, she has created a space in which South Asian women of color can speak of things that are often considered taboo in South Asian culture, such as their sexuality, insecurities, and sexual assaults.

Through her willingness to be vulnerable, and choosing to not filter her thoughts and feelings, she has emerged from the pain of her past and has connected with millions of people across the world with her poetry. She has inspired conversations on how women should take ownership of their own bodies, and how communities throughout the world need to open conversations on the taboo subjects that perpetuate negative stigmas and poor mental health.

One of the worst parts of being authentic is having to prepare yourself for criticism and accepting people will dislike you for no reason. This can be difficult for women, who are primed to be people pleasers and are taught other people's opinions of them matter greatly from a young age. In fact, the entire beauty industry was built upon making women feel as though they need to perform certain behaviors or buy certain products to alter themselves in some ways—that they're simply not good enough as they are.

This mentality bleeds into many other sectors of society as well. Women are constantly told from childhood that they need to act, look, and dress a certain way, often to please other people rather than themselves. A study on the treatment of male versus female children in schools found that while boys were told to stop negative behaviors, they were rarely advised on alternative ways to act. Girls, however, were often given specific instructions on how to act, such as "sit up straight and speak softly."[129] While industries and other institutions may be changing with breakthrough companies/organizations that promote self-acceptance, it will take decades to undo the history of making women feel they must cater to other people.

Brené Brown, a respected research professor and expert on vulnerability and shame, has previously declared that "authenticity is a collection of choices that we have to make every day," demonstrating it's not a one-off decision but rather a continuous, active effort.[130] It comes with accepting your strengths and weaknesses and understanding that no matter how hard you try, you will never completely feel ready to go after your greatest goals and dreams.

---

129   William A. Corsaro, *The Sociology of Childhood*, (Los Angeles: SAGE Publications, 2010), 209.

130   Brené Brown, *The Gifts of Imperfection: Let Go of Who You Think You're Supposed to Be and Embrace Who You Are* (Center City: Hazelden, 2010).

When I was on the phone with Suhani, I found myself unexpectedly pouring out my feelings of inadequacy into the conversation. Here I was, interviewing a phenomenal young woman for a book I was set to publish, and I still felt like I wasn't qualified to be an author. "Sometimes I find myself wondering if I should have even embarked on this journey at all," I confided in her. "After interviewing and learning about so many women who have done amazing things, they all seem to have something...special. I don't know if I have that yet. Maybe I should have waited a few years to develop that kind of perspective on the world, to gain more experiences..." I trailed off.

Rather than laugh at me, Suhani gently gave me some tough love. "You're waiting for some universal thing—that time never comes!" she exclaimed. "Even if it seems like perfect timing, maybe it's really not! I was never intending to start something, and if I had thought critically about starting Myna, I would have never done it at the time. Thank God I didn't think about critically about it!" she laughed, and immediately I was at ease again. She reminded me that rather than give up, we need to struggle through and stay in the game. "Go ahead and do it, knowing that it will be challenging," she urged me. "Being in the challenge and doing it versus anticipating obstacles and not doing it—even if you aren't successful, you will learn something out of it."

My conversation with Suhani made me realize how easy it is to psyche yourself out of pursuing your goals. But nothing worth having ever comes easy. It doesn't matter how prepared or unprepared we feel because we'll always have some unexpected obstacle to overcome. Maybe you didn't account for a certain challenge, or maybe the people who always claimed to be by your side start disappearing as you begin to embrace the person you truly are. This realization may lead one to feel isolated and alone, or scared to show their true interests, passions, and talents.

However, you have unique talents and ideas that will better the world. When you're authentically yourself, you will inspire people everywhere you meet. Rather than hide your individuality, own it. Weak points don't have to be hidden; rather, if they're acknowledged, they can serve as the bridges that connect you with others. There's no need to consider personality traits as "masculine" or "feminine"—they can simply be left alone as gender-neutral characteristics. It's very difficult to resist succumbing to societal norms, to refuse to hide in the shadows of everyone else you meet. But when you decide to step into the light, to not apologize for who you are, people are drawn to that. The right people will surround you, and your future will be that much brighter.

CHAPTER 6

ADVERSITY

———

I realize I occupy a place of privilege. And yet I continue to face challenges every day, simply because I am a woman.

I walk through my esteemed campus, only to enter rooms where people believe I'm too emotional to discuss health care policy with clarity. When I express that my micro-economics problem set is challenging, usually because of the math involved, offhand comments ensue, attributing it to my gender's inability to handle more "difficult subjects." Some days my friends and I meet up in the city, and I have to walk back to my car alone. I automatically avoid shaded areas, thread my keys through my fingers, and have my friend on the phone to make me feel less on edge. If a man catcalls me, I hide my disgust, and sometimes fear, by carefully constructing a neutral expression, holding my back straight, and straining my ears to make sure I don't hear footsteps following me. Even though I deserve the right to hold space and be respected, many others want to make me feel small, just because they don't believe women deserve to be seen or heard.

But while this may be intimidating to acknowledge, women across the world have demonstrated we have the power to not only survive but flourish amid these obstacles. Every female changemaker who has created a positive impact had to rise above the challenges they faced, even if it seemed impossible at the time.

Even though our society makes moves toward gender equality every day, centuries of cultural norms cannot be changed instantly. In many countries around the world, women do a majority of unpaid labor, such as housekeeping and caring for children and the elderly, yet still suffer from the gender wage gap and struggle to bring back as much income as their male counterparts.[131]

Even from countries with the highest male contributions to domestic work, men at most only spend 63 percent as much time on unpaid domestic work as women.[132] In rural parts of Africa, women spend 40 billion hours a year collecting water because freshwater resources tend to be far, and they often have to travel on foot in intense heat for hours to collect enough water for their families every day.[133]

While men are just as capable, cultural norms have assigned this task to women, and without systems that will promote

131 "Economic Inequality Across Gender Diversity," Inequality.org, Institute for Policy Studies, accessed June 8, 2020.

132 Ibid.

133 Inter-Agency Task Force on Rural Women, "Facts & Figures: Rural Women and the Millennium Development Goals," UN WomenWatch, accessed June 8, 2020.

change in gender norms, it's difficult for women to break out of such norms without putting their families at risk. Only six countries in the world give women the same legal work rights as men; a majority of economies often at most grant three-quarters the rights as men in similar measured areas.[134] Every day, around 33,000 girls become child brides before they've reached the age of eighteen.[135] In many cases, these girls are not culturally valued as highly as boys are in their communities. So when you're poor, marrying off your young daughter makes good financial sense; the transaction passes the "economic burden" to another family. In the United States, one in five women will be raped at some point in their lives.[136] Depending on the country, up to 70 percent of women will have experienced physical and/or sexual violence in their lifetimes.[137]

With women encountering obstacles at every forefront of their lives, it demonstrates how difficult it can be for women

134 Women, Business, and the Law, *Workplace, 2020,* The World Bank, accessed June 8, 2020.

135 "Child Marriage Around the World," Girls Not Brides, accessed June 8, 2020.

136 Michele C. Black et al., *The National Intimate Partner and Sexual Violence Survey (NISVS): 2010 Summary Report,* National Center for Injury Prevention and Control, Centers for Disease Control and Prevention, November 2011.

137 Claudia García-Moreno et al., "Global and Regional Estimates of Violence against Women: Prevalence and Health Effects of Intimate Partner Violence And Non-Partner Sexual Violence," Department of Reproductive Health and Research, World Health Organization, ed. Penny Howes, 2013.

to convince other people to shift the power balance, let alone empower themselves. Though the situation may seem dire, millions of women have successfully carved out their own paths, risen above challenges, and lifted not only themselves out of such circumstances but other women as well.

When asked about the core aspects of a female change-maker, Dr. Christi Navarro, a community health professor at Nova Southeastern University, explained everyone has faced some type of adversity in their lifetime. In most cases, they've experienced or witnessed some type of trauma, but the value comes in how they let this experience move them into insisting upon change.

When people imagine adversity, they often think of the most extreme cases: Malala being threatened and attacked by the Taliban, girls miraculously escaping from forced marriages, refugees escaping war-torn countries and becoming separated from their families, people who survive natural disasters yet must watch their homes become destroyed in front of their eyes. It's not wrong to immediately think of these cases. They are miraculous in their own right and often are the subject of media coverage, documentaries, and the stories we hear at global conferences.

Adversity comes in all shapes and sizes. Everyone's lives present different challenges, and your own challenges shouldn't be diminished just because someone else is suffering more. It's always valuable to keep things in perspective, but no matter your position and privileges, you will always face struggles and have obstacles to overcome.

Facing adversity from within can also create roadblocks for success. Elyse Fox knows a thing or two about these roadblocks. Her lifelong battle with depression started as a child, and she struggled to find any information on mental health issues. As she noted a huge lack of resources for women of color, it became difficult to get the support she needed. From what she could see, no advocates were successful amid their mental illness. The Brooklyn-born filmmaker chose to release a short film about her struggle with depression, entitled "Conversations with Friends."[138] What followed would change the trajectory of her life; she received an outpouring of messages from young women who connected with her struggles.

Elyse saw a need, so she rose up to create the Sad Girls Club, a safe space for people to talk about their emotional struggles among a supportive community of others experiencing similar challenges. This organization has helped chip away at the stigma surrounding mental health and has provided a beacon of light for many young women of color.

In an interview with Health.com, she admired the impact of what she has created, saying, "It's so beautiful to me...to make new history about the way we talk about mental health."[139] By taking hold of the power of her own struggles, of her own story, she has allowed thousands of other women the

---

138 Sarah Klein, "This Instagram Activist Is Smashing the Stigma on Depression: 'I Want to Change the Narrative of a Picture-Perfect life,'" Health. com, May 29, 2018.

139 Ibid.

freedom to heal by opening up about their own challenges in a judgment-free space.

Meanwhile, on the other side of the world, a then eighteen-year-old Litia Baleilevuka was about to have her eyes opened to the vast effects of climate change. As Cyclone Winston destroyed villages on Fiji, Litia bore witness to the destruction of thousands of lives and homes, and in the wake of the brutal storm, Litia rose up to become a climate activist. Climate change was no longer just a theory for her. Rising sea levels had threatened her home, and extreme weather events had destroyed her family's ancestral islands beyond repair. When I got the chance to interview Litia, she recounted those first moments when she saw her mother's village after the cyclone had hit.

"My mom's village got completely decimated. All that remained were the foundations of the houses—there was nothing else left."

Litia described the scene as appearing as though someone had taken a plow to the village and upturned the ground underneath it. I couldn't fathom what it must have felt like to watch helplessly as the place where you grew up was swept away in an instant. This is where she had celebrated holidays, where she had played, where she knew every individual home and family. She told me how Fiji is a very communal society, where everyone's considered family even if they're not blood-related.

"When I [saw] what had happened to their homes," she continued, "when I [saw] that something I felt would always be there [could] be easily taken away within a night, within a couple of hours, it hit me quite hard." She chose to use the experience to advocate for action. She became an activist for Pacific Island Represent and has spoken about climate change both locally and internationally. In 2018, at the COP24 climate change conference in Poland, she shared how Cyclone Winston had forced thousands of people to not only lose their homes but also their loved ones and livelihoods.

Litia, like many other climate activists, calls out polluting companies for the emissions they discharge because the effects of such pollution hit smaller countries like Fiji the hardest. Even though she could have let fear paralyze her, she now implements climate mitigation projects so that people can begin to build their lives back up.

Being from a small country like Fiji, it would have been easy for her to be intimidated, to refrain from joining in the global conversation, because many people would refuse to listen to someone so young. Many small countries are often left out of conversations about climate change because larger countries control many of the resources they need, so challenging the status quo could potentially affect their livelihood.

Litia has been challenged on all levels: from her household, to her community, to the global policymakers that won't take concrete action. Yet she has remained steadfast in her dedication and continues to educate others patiently, even focusing on capacity building recently to better equip herself for these conversations.

"There's value in being able to know and understand, in being able to empathize with your audience. At the end of the day, awareness is very important, but it's also important to act upon this awareness, which I think is lacking now. There's been a lot of reactive responses, or people waiting for something to happen, which is not realistic. For island countries, especially, we can't wait for it to start happening, or for the bigger countries to act. The truth is if we don't start, our lands won't be around."

Slowly but surely, she's found ways to help communicate the importance of climate action and has worked hard to create change and help her communities continue to fight. Litia has demonstrated adversity is experienced by people of all ages, and all have the right to have their story heard, no matter where you come from or how old you are.

When you look at Elyse and Litia, it's easier to list their differences rather than their similarities. Their stories have very little overlap, and they're advocating for completely different causes. Even their personal stories are so different: Elyse's battle was mainly internal and lasted years, while Litia had her world turned upside down by one extreme event. But looking deeper into their experiences, you can see that even though these two young women have experienced very different lives and struggles, both have spread vital messages. And those messages have helped many people rise above their challenges and use the stories of their own struggles to promote change.

Deja Foxx is used to adversity, as her very platform for advocacy, unfortunately, invites it. Advocating for reproductive rights would never be easy considering it's a contentious subject across the globe. But as a young woman of color coming from a background of poverty, Deja has had constant naysayers and obstacles placed in her path as she fights for Planned Parenthood to keep its funding.

Yet she hasn't let the challenges keep her from achieving her goals and setting new ones. She even appreciates adversity and spoke about it in her interview with GirlTalk HQ in 2016. "Through adversity, I have become a powerful woman," she stated. "Feeling as though I had nothing taught me that my story and voice were things that could never be taken away or silenced."[140] She went on to explain how the difficult circumstances she faced helped her develop a sense of empathy, which she cited as her "greatest strength."[141] Deja understood the ability to draw upon her own experiences and the experiences of others allowed her to create positive change, where she believes her true power comes from.

I used to constantly be in turmoil about my desire for social change. Even though I'd faced my fair share of challenges growing up, I still have privileges that have been denied to many. How would I even be welcomed into the spaces I wanted to work in? Would people even believe I was being sincere? One of the greatest challenges to social change can be ourselves. I have learned that even though I've been fortunate enough to a level of privilege, I can still advocate and

---

140 Deja Foxx, "Exclusive Interview with Deja Foxx – Teen Activist, Change-Maker, & Future Political Leader," interview by Asha Dahya, *GirlTalkHQ*, April 27, 2017.

141 Ibid.

do sincerely create social impact. It's about carving out my space and acknowledging that I belong there; I had to believe I was in the place I was meant to be, and that I deserved to be there. I can use my experiences to connect with others and transform that energy into impact.

The ability to transform adversity into strength is one of the most powerful trademarks of the female changemakers we see today. It is not the absence of adversity that allows success but the perseverance and reflection on such experiences that allow women to rise and draw upon them to spread their message more effectively. By understanding challenges are a part of the path to change, it will be easier to accept them and strategize on how to overcome them as they are encountered. When it comes to making a change, learn to make adversity the steppingstone to success.

CHAPTER 7

RESILIENCE

———

"You're too pretty to become a doctor!"

"You're wasting your parents' money on a college degree when you'll just get married off."

"This industry is a boys' club."

"Oh really? That's a little ambitious to think you could do that, isn't it?"

"Men are mentally stronger than women."

When I asked my friends on a random Tuesday morning to send me a few examples of gender microaggressions they've heard, I expected maybe three or four people to respond. I couldn't have prepared myself for the barrage of messages from friends all over the country. For some, the question triggered painful memories. "Just typing those out made me angry!" a friend exclaimed when I called her. "Can we never catch a break?"

Before we even begin our careers, we receive the message loud and clear: expect to work twice as hard to be taken seriously. In my own life, I've found no matter how much I accomplish, some people will doubt my capabilities and want me to make myself smaller.

When I express that I want to become a leader in health implementation strategies, classmates say it's too hard for someone of my "background" to attain that kind of success. I watch as my male peers receive undivided attention when they're speaking at a presentation and then witness the same formerly attentive listeners become disinterested and side-tracked before I can even open my mouth. I've been told I shouldn't be too loud, too bold, or too different, because what kind of family would want that in a daughter-in-law? I've hit wall after wall, and sometimes I don't want to pick myself back up after so much opposition. But even when I get tired, there is a reason I force myself to keep going. Every woman I look up to emphasizes the importance of being resilient.

Resilience is one of the core principles of being a female changemaker; without it, no change can be accomplished. It is necessary because challenges are inevitable, and how you respond to such challenges is the key to how change is created. While we may like to fantasize that our path to creating a positive impact would be met with complete agreement and support, in reality, no valuable change is made that doesn't encounter opposition to some degree.

This principle is made up of several characteristics—working in conjunction to create a more resilient individual. Without cultivating these characteristics, resolve can be easily broken. It's vital to understand change-making is not always about success; obstacles and failure are also key parts of the process. Without knowing how to respond to the inevitable challenges of change-making, it can be difficult to create the impact one desires.

Building resilience begins with self-awareness, because without knowing who you are and your strengths/weaknesses, you're not accounting for the obstacles you may present to yourself as you start your journey to create change.

SELF-AWARENESS

How well do you know yourself? It seems like a trivial question; how could you not know yourself? Yet there is a strong basis for this question. Tasha Eurich, an organizational psychologist, conducted a series of surveys to explore how many people were self-aware—that is, how well did they think they knew themselves.

In her book, *Insight*, she reveals that when surveyed, 95 percent of people believed they were self-aware, when in reality, only 12–15 percent actually were.[142] In her words, this discrepancy means a shocking truth: "On a good day, about 80 percent of people are lying about themselves—to themselves."[143] She attributes this to three key factors: our

142 Tasha Eurich, *Insight: The Surprising Truth about How Others See Us, How We See Ourselves, and Why the Answers Matter More Than We Think* (New York: Crown, 2017).

143 Tasha Eurich, "The Importance of Self-Awareness with Tasha Eurich," interviewed by Chad Gordon, *Blanchard LeaderChat*, February 1, 2019.

natural blind spots, the feel-good effect (where we seek to see ourselves in a more positive light), and the increase in self-absorbed mindsets with the explosion of social media.[144]

But what's the problem with this? After all, when we think of those who are self-aware, we reserve the characteristic for the old and wise—the people who have been around long enough to take the time to know themselves. How can a young person who is constantly evolving be self-aware? With every year that passes, it usually becomes harder to recognize who they previously were. But Eurich believes there's more value to self-awareness than on a personal level; she believes it is an essential skill, and her research has shown it is the foundation of many positives in life, such as lasting relationships, high performance, and smart choices.[145]

Self-awareness can be elusive if one doesn't pay attention because it often requires confronting and acknowledging both the ideal and less-than-ideal aspects of yourself. It requires not only being conscious of your character but also your feelings, which can be uncomfortable for most people, especially regarding anything negative. Yet self-awareness is not a stand-alone process; it is the first step to creating a deeper understanding of yourself. By understanding your weaknesses, you can focus on tapping into your strengths and actively work to account for these self-created obstacles.

---

144 Jeff Kauflin, "Only 15% of People Are Self-Aware — Here's How to Change," *Forbes*, May 10, 2017.

145 Eurich, "The Importance of Self-Awareness with Tasha Eurich."

No one can simply wake up and just become self-aware; there's no inner switch to turn on that will automatically give you all the answers. In fact, there are two types of self-awareness: internal and external. According to Eurich, internal awareness is what we commonly think of; it's the consciousness of your values, aspirations, strengths, and weaknesses.[146] External awareness is knowing how other people perceive you. Both are mutually exclusive qualities, as it's possible to score high in one area and low on the other. But the key to self-awareness is that it can be developed. All that is needed is the willingness to improve and some effort.

For example, one of the most critical elements of becoming self-aware is asking for feedback. It's rare to find someone who enjoys hearing feedback from others; it places you in a vulnerable position and often can conflict with our own perception of ourselves, our work, our intentions, etc. But sitting in the discomfort of the activity, understanding it will help you grow as a person and identify the areas for improvement you couldn't determine for yourself, will prove it to be an invaluable process.

Even the most objectively successful people in this world believe in the power of feedback. Bill Gates himself said, "We all need people who give us feedback. That's how we improve."[147] However, you don't necessarily need to seek out harsh criticism. Eurich suggests finding a "loving critic," someone who wants you to be successful but will

---

146 Ibid.

147 Bill Gates, "Teachers Need Real Feedback," Filmed May 2013 in New York, NY, TED Video, 00:31.

not sugarcoat the truth.[148] This specific combination of factors will allow you to face reality without destroying your self-confidence.

Internal awareness can sometimes be even more difficult to cultivate. The best route may not be by conducting an in-depth self-analysis through long journal entries or abstractly looking for the hidden meanings behind your thoughts and actions. Rather, the simplest things usually yield the most profound self-discoveries. What makes work fulfilling? What motivates you to achieve your goals? What are your long-term goals?

While sometimes the answers from yourself, and others, can initially cause a negative reaction, it's important to recognize this is a part of the process of becoming conscious about yourself. As Marianne Williamson said in her book, *A Return to Love*, "It takes courage…to endure the sharp pains of self-discovery rather than choose to take the dull pain of unconsciousness that would last the rest of our lives."[149]

While it may seem like a lofty sentiment, understanding you're not all-knowing and you won't be the best at everything helps you learn humility and how to be respectful of others when facing their flaws and strengths. If you want to be a great leader, other people will only want to follow you if you present yourself accurately, and that starts with knowing yourself completely.

---

148 Kauflin, "Only 15% of People Are Self-Aware — Here's How to Change."

149 Marianne Williamson, *A Return to Love: Reflections on the Principles of "A Course in Miracles"* (New York: Harper Collins, 2009).

Dorota Sobieszczuk found self-awareness was key in becoming an effective leader. The Polish co-founder of The Good Cards, a real-life game that helps organizations and individuals achieve collective goals to create a better world, understands unlocking leadership potential within others starts with knowing yourself.[150] In her own life, a leadership development program helped her realize the importance of self-awareness, as she encountered various struggles in leading the team she was given.

In an interview with Better World International, she recounts how a conflict in the management style of her team made her realize her past had caused her to push herself and others in a very demanding and results-driven way. She learned she couldn't lead people well if she didn't take care of herself, and now believes self-awareness is "essential for growth as a human."[151] Sobieszczuk's experience demonstrates the power that our past and personality can have on others if we don't recognize the roots of our behaviors, but also that once you take steps toward self-awareness, you can create opportunities for a better future.

ACCEPTANCE OF FAILURE

It's interesting, isn't it? That one of the intrinsic parts of success is the darkest moment you'll go through: failure. How many of us want to admit we've failed before, especially in

---

150 Dorota Sobieszczuk, "How to Find Your Inner Change-Maker: Story of Dorota," interviewed by Corey Harnish, *Better World International*, July 11, 2017.

151 Ibid.

something we really wanted? It's a hard outcome to deal with as an individual, and we're even less inclined to let others know. After all, we live in a world where everyone only shares their successes and the highlights of their life. Everyone has struggles, so who wants to see that when we're trying to escape them through social media and the internet? Wouldn't it kill the illusion of perfection for our role models and idols if we knew they, like the rest of us, have experienced failure countless times?

The answer is yes. It would kill the perfect image of the people we look up to. But the question we should be asking instead is why do we hold our leaders and role models to a standard of perfection? Why is failure considered "imperfect" when it is present in every single person's life?

The truth is no one will win every battle. Women, especially, will experience many moments of frustration and sadness because people will actively work against the rights we deserve. Some people will invalidate our arguments, feelings, and experiences simply because that's how they were brought up and/or the mentality they've maintained. Not every person will support you, even if asked nicely or even if you consider your cause flawless.

Andrea Alejandra Gonzales, a passionate advocate for the end of gun violence, had her life shaken up when the Parkland school shooting occurred in 2018, the same year in which she was a senior in high school. "After Parkland, I was really shaken," she explained to me in an interview. "The moment I heard about it, I felt a visceral reaction. It was especially hard for me because I was a senior. I had a college picked out, my prom dress ready, and here were these young people who had this same future completely demolished in front of them within moments."

A few weeks later, a copycat attempted to replicate a similar fear, and her school was on lockdown for a few hours. She remembers the fear that permeated the air. Her heart pounded with every passing moment, thinking of her younger sister who was just a freshman at the same school. Seeing her teacher, who she looked up to, start crying was a very important moment, mainly because it was so hard for her to watch.

Andrea realized she needed to do something and organized a school walkout with several friends to raise awareness on the issue of gun violence. That walkout, which comprised over a thousand students, propelled her into her current path of being an activist. Now the director of operations at Youth Over Guns and the director of community and youth engagement at New Yorkers Against Gun Violence, she has used her experiences to propel herself right into the world of advocacy and activism. She's become passionate about gender equity, racial justice work, and decolonization, and puts her all in everything she does.

But while she is on the path to success, she shared a time when she confronted her first major "failure" in the space. In 2018, a distressing event appeared in the news; a young Black activist named Danye Jones was found hanging from a tree in his backyard. Enormous controversy followed, as the medical examiner ruled it a suicide, but his friends, family, and activist community suspected he was lynched due to his involvement in the Ferguson protests.[152]

Andrea recounts the time when she heard this news and felt incredibly distressed by it. "When any type of violence happens, I feel severely impacted and want to even curl up in a ball about it. But I remember someone convinced me to do some type of event to help raise awareness on the systemic issues that contributed to this horrible act. I didn't ask for help and chose to do it all on my own, and in my eyes, it fell through because it didn't have the impact that I wanted it to have."

"I was upset that I couldn't do better for him or for that community, and I was upset that I couldn't be a better organizer," she confided in me. But Andrea also gave me insight into how she was able to use the experience to move on from this point. "Failure is such a strong word because there's always something that can be learned," she acknowledged. "I think about the conversations that I had, and how I learned who were my allies along with my strengths and weaknesses." She learned to redefine the meaning of success and reimagine the concept of failure. "These conversations and the chance to learn about myself was a success, even if I couldn't see it at the time." Using Andrea's perspective, we can look at these inevitable "failures" as building blocks to a better future.

Luckily, some people have recognized the importance of emphasizing failure as part of the journey to success and

---

152 Joe Penney, "The Fight for Justice Takes Its Toll on Ferguson Activists," *New York Review Daily*, February 12, 2019.

are creating programs that even encourage it. Cristal Glang-chai, author of *Venture Girls* and founder/CEO of VentureLab, realized that for young women especially, it was important to create an environment where failure was not just accepted, but welcomed. VentureLab seeks to run experiential learning programs for young people interested in tech entrepreneurship.[153]

In the VentureLab curricula, she builds failure into the lesson plans. In a post for the website Quartz at Work, she explains how this method encourages young girls to try new ideas, build past their skill set, and take a chance at things that may not work.[154] Lo and behold, they often don't work! But the value of this environment that celebrates failure allows girls to break down the fear of it.

We should encourage the philosophy that failure is healthy and still relays valuable information about what doesn't work. After all, as Bryant McGill wrote in his book, *Simple Reminders*, "Rejection is merely a redirection."[155] If one wants to successfully champion change, it starts with understanding setbacks don't have to hinder growth and progress; they merely delay it slightly. It's imperative that we, as a society, learn to be more open and honest about the goals that weren't met, the naysayers, the struggles we've experienced, etc., to

---

153 "Meet Dr. Glangchai," VentureGirls, accessed June 8, 2020.

154 Cristal Glangchai, "The Importance of Showing Girls It's OK to Fail," *Quartz*, April 26, 2018.

155 Bryant McGill, *Simple Reminders: Inspiration for Living Your Best Life* (SRN, 2015).

create a more holistic view on what success truly looks like and how it is actually achieved.

PATIENCE

Change is seldom instant; it usually follows a constant uphill battle. In most cases, it will take years to get a movement going, to create any type of impact. This is because not only can it be difficult to gather the resources to create change, but also due to the many institutional barriers that often provide obstacles to progress.

According to the National Institute for Women and Information Technology, institutional barriers are "policies, procedures, or situations that systematically disadvantage certain groups of people."[156] Often most present in majority-minority situations, they can range from racism, sexism, age discrimination, and more. Barriers such as these often take an unassuming disposition, often qualified with statements such as "this is normal" or "this is how it's always been done." In most cases, people often believe it's impossible to challenge these barriers, as they're too intertwined with daily life. If it's worked for this long, what's the point of changing it?

Yet this is not a case of "if it's not broken, don't fix it." The existence of institutional barriers demonstrates a need for changes to be made. It shows people are being excluded or receiving unequal access to resources, opportunities, and

---

156   "Institutional Barriers & Their Effects: How Can I Talk to Colleagues about These Issues?" National Center for Women and Information Technology, May 6, 2009.

rights. When attempting to create change, expect it to take months, years, or even decades for changes to be made and implemented.

While it can seem discouraging to imagine you may not be able to see the impact you desire according to your own timeline, plenty of young women are working toward spreading positive change, even though it is slow moving and is taking years to make progress. Any female changemaker can attest to the fact that their movement started years ago, even if they only recently started getting media coverage. In the world of creating impact, there's no such thing as an overnight sensation.

A phenomenal example of patience can be attributed to one female changemaker who has already spent years advocating for climate change: Xiye Bastida. As a Mexican-Chilean immigrant who also comes from an Otomi-Toltec background, Xiye has acquired a vast knowledge of the history of indigenous communities in terms of climate activism and advocating for change.

I asked Xiye to provide her insight on this specific space and topic. "Indigenous communities have different experiences around the world; these experiences are all different, but none of them are really good," she told me. She listed the many pressing social issues that plague these communities— substance abuse, murder, missing indigenous women—but they consistently always ask for one thing: respect the earth and please take care of it. "All we're asking is that you align your hearts with us and protect the earth. It is about our morals, values, and what we believe as truth."

Indigenous communities have struggled with having companies and governments encroach upon their land for centuries. They will resort to stealing, displacing, and/or pressuring community members to give it up or allow the construction of pipelines, buildings, and more.[157] But Xiye told me about the philosophy she had been taught, which she still holds today. "We need to take care of the earth. There's this idea of reciprocity; the earth gives us so much, so all it asks in return is that we respect and protect it." While she grew up in a small town that upheld this philosophy, they, unfortunately, couldn't escape the effects of the climate crisis.

The day before her family was set to leave for New York for her parents' new job opportunities, her hometown of San Pedro Tultepec was flooded by a neighboring river considered a waste dump by a nearby factory. The contaminants spread all over the land, and Xiye barely had time to process before she found herself in New York City. There, as she observed the area, she realized climate change was affecting communities everywhere. But rather than focus on blaming the consumer for their actions, Xiye pushed the students at her school to advocate for structural change and lobby politicians. Her efforts have gotten bills passed, she's organized school strikes, testified at City Hall, and been interviewed by many different platforms to spread her message and story.

Unsurprisingly, Xiye and her fellow climate activists have had countless people invalidate their efforts due to their age. During our conversation, Xiye described a comment made at

---

157 "Climate Change," Department of Economic and Social Affairs, United Nations, accessed June 8, 2020.

a panel she was on at COP25. The journalist directed a blunt set of questions to the panel of five young activists. "COP has been around for twenty-five years, so why do you kids think you can come here and say something different? What's so special about you guys? What can you say that hasn't been said for the past twenty-five years? Why do you think you can change anything?"

Xiye couldn't believe they needed to defend their credibility. Here they were, organizing efforts across their communities, missing precious days of school, and they were at this conference because they cared about the cause and had chosen to act. Rather than become angry, Xiye chose to answer the question with dignity. "I think that the world has never been at this point ever before," she responded. "As the climate crisis gets worse, you're going to get more climate activists. Everybody's action toward one collective action will lead to change. We have to keep going."

"But you're just kids," the journalist countered. "You're not going to do anything!"

Rather than take the bait, Xiye decided to convey a serious answer with a little lightheartedness. "When you give students a deadline, they know they have to get something done. They've given us ours, and we have ten years." After hearing her response, the reporter backed down, but Xiye knew the journalist likely remained unconvinced. She expressed this concern later in the interview.

"It worries me that people still don't understand my motivation for being a climate activist," she remarked a little wearily.

"I'm doing this because I don't want this world to flood and burn. This is already happening and it's going to get worse. I'm not doing this for me; I'm doing this for all of us!" It frustrates her, as people see the climate crisis as an opinion rather than a fact to act upon.

Amid all these obstacles, Xiye has refused to give up. She has continued the struggle to make climate change a priority. While she demands change be made immediately, she also understands most change will not be instantaneous. Climate change action is a very slow-moving process, and usually difficult for people, especially those who don't bear the brunt effects of the issue, to realize their own agency in the problem and potential solution. It's especially made difficult by the companies who refuse to take ownership of the damage they're creating, as they don't wish to sacrifice their profits for the betterment of the environment.[158]

Yet Xiye does not look back on the centuries of struggle for these marginalized communities as a reason to give up; she looks to them as an example of perseverance. "I think of the struggles that have endured beforehand. A few years is nothing compared to what my family has been through, what my community has been through. If our struggles make the world a better place, it's worth it."

While it continues to be an upward battle, her efforts have paid off slowly but surely. Not only has she spoken on international platforms and gained support from people of all

---

158   Jo Confino, "Report Shows Companies Still Don't Take Climate Change Seriously," *The Guardian*, September 12, 2013.

backgrounds, but she was honored with the "Spirit of the UN" award in 2018. She continues with the climate strike as an organizer for Fridays for Future. She is a member of the administration committee of the Peoples Climate Movement, where she has brought the voice of youth to existing climate and grassroots organizations. She also is a coordinator for the Re-Earth Initiative, which hopes to make climate change accessible to all people through "uplifting voices of those who have been historically marginalized, and frontline communities."[159]

Xiye's work in creating awareness about the climate crisis has helped hundreds of thousands of people and various nations become more eco-conscious. For example, single-use plastics are being phased out throughout the world; Taiwan even announced an all-inclusive ban on plastic bags, straws, utensils, etc., hoping to completely phase them out by 2030.[160]

While we may be unable to directly correlate these changes to Xiye, she likely helped ignite and sustain the passion for climate change among many people. Xiye Bastida demonstrates how, while we should demand change be made now to convey its urgency, it's beneficial to be patient and not get discouraged when it takes longer than expected to make a positive impact.

---

159 "Meet the Team," The Re-Earth Initiative, accessed June 8, 2020.

160 Xavier Sun, "Taiwan Soon to be Plastic Free," *Waste Not Asia* 1, no. 1 (2018): 16-20.

PERSEVERANCE

Jihye Yang was like any other girl in South Korea. She would go to class, sit quietly in frustration as female classmates were told to "act and dress modestly," watch in silent disgust as teachers called out specific students to judge their appearance, and then go home and wonder what she could do about the situation. Male classmates created group texts to rate the bodies of their female peers, and when the teachers found out, they often faced no repercussions. While this isn't the case for all schools in South Korea, it was a reality Yang had to deal with in hers. She had heard about illegal filming cases, with secret cameras filming women in homes, on streets, on toilets, in motels, etc.[161] With all these injustices being committed against women every day, what could one girl do to make a change?

Yang soon decided on a path of activism at the age of sixteen and has now become a co-representative of youth organization Teenager Feminist Network WeTee. With the arrival of the international #MeToo movement, which is attempting to break the stigma surrounding sexual violence survivors, she helped bring the movement into more schools and groups.[162] Through her organization of feminist groups and protests, she allowed more girls the chance to speak against the sexual abuse and discrimination they have faced. Yang has helped create a cultural shift in which more young women identify as feminists and now will actively fight against patriarchal standards within South Korea.

---

161 Jessie Yeung, Erin Chan and Michelle Lim, "Young People Across Asia Pushed for Change in 2019. Meet Five of Them," CNN, December 26, 2019.

162 "History and Vision," Me Too Movement, accessed June 8, 2020.

She has called upon the South Korean government to address the issue of sexual harassment and discrimination yet felt they didn't give a substantial response. Rather than give up, she went directly to the United Nations in 2018. At the Convention on the Rights of the Child, she discussed this movement that fought against such harassment and elaborated on how it discriminated against women and young women immensely. While it took time, her relentless efforts did result in progress being made. The South Korean Ministry of Education set up a gender equality team and the first official channel for student victims to report sexual abuse. While it wasn't executed perfectly, as students weren't sent any information about how to use the channel, it indicated a start in the right direction.[163]

The core principle that goes right alongside patience is perseverance. Dr. Kimberly K. Merriman, a performance management researcher, believes strongly in the importance of perseverance for leaders. She details how "perseverance is a human quality associated with exceptional leaders in a variety of domains."[164] Successful female changemakers are committed to their cause; no matter how many battles they may face, they will get up and continue to push for what they believe is right. They may reinvent, or redesign their plan of attack, but they will never forget their mission.

Jihye Yang realized what she was fighting for would not come easy. Sexual violence, assault, and discrimination topics tend to lead to victim-blaming, and most governments would

163   Yeung, Chan, and Lim, "Young People across Asia..."

164   Kimberly Merriman, *Leadership and Perseverance,* 2017.

rather remain uninvolved than take a direct stance or create actionable policies to address these issues. Regardless, Yang recognized the value in the struggle and was committed to not leaving things as they were.

As Yang has demonstrated, social change is a long and arduous process. Mobilizing people and institutions to effect policies or alter negative stereotypes takes countless efforts that often fall flat. For every small win, a dozen failures trail behind it. Fortunately, perseverance isn't simply an innate trait; it can be fostered if one is given the right direction.

ACVEO, a UK-based organization that aims to inspire and support civil society leaders by providing connections, advocacy, and skills, believes perseverance starts with simply maintaining a commitment to your vision.[165] As ACVEO Trustee Sue Tibballs relays in an article on habits of successful changemakers, "You cannot persist if there is constant internal pressure to change priorities, so the change you are seeking needs to make sense to everyone."[166]

This is not the same as catering your goals to what others may want; it's about learning how to clearly articulate what you aim to do so everyone is on the same page. By clarifying your goals to others, it becomes easier to gain long-term support as you move toward demanding and implementing social change. Also, valuing perseverance itself will make it easier to resist changing your approach/method to social impact

---

165 "About," ACVEO, accessed June 8, 2020.

166 Sue Tibballs, "12 Habits of Successful Change-Makers: Persistence, Perseverance & Resilience," ACVEO, April 18, 2019.

to something that is "fresh" or will incite media coverage. By encouraging not only yourself but your supporters, as well, to persevere in face of obstacles and setbacks, you set a precedent to becoming a resilient leader and changemaker, and you'll inspire dedication and commitment to your cause as well.

FOCUS

For many women, being unable to save or help every person is a crippling thought. Those advocating for change, for resources, or for the rights of others, can especially take it as a personal failure if they can't reach or help people in time. Unfortunately, with limited time, money, resources, and reach, it's impossible for one person to save an entire population in need. However, this shouldn't be a debilitating realization that stops us from trying altogether. There is still value in one life, in helping those you can, because without you, they wouldn't have been helped at all.

As I was researching young female activists and leaders, I was graciously pointed in the direction of Imxn Abdul. Imxn is one of the founding members of Integrate NYC, an organization that pushes to integrate the New York City public school system. When I spoke with Imxn, her bubbly nature shone through the screen from the moment she said hello. But when it came to her work with the organization and the reason why she started this journey in the first place, she got down to business and offered insight on her journey without hesitation.

Imxn was a high school senior when she learned New York City has the most segregated school system in the United States. While she was initially shocked at the news, she reflected on her own experience growing up, remembering how her mother used to drive her twenty to twenty-five minutes away from home to attend a "better" school, and how she, as a result, often did not see many students of color alongside her. In her predominantly white high school, she struggled to find her place as a biracial young woman of Lebanese and Puerto Rican descent. "We had to build cultural clubs as safe spaces," she revealed to me. "At school, we often didn't feel safe, recognized, and we were often silenced when we voiced our concerns."

During her senior year, she was introduced to Sarah Camiscoli, who taught in the South Bronx. She had created Integrate NYC as an elective class in her high school, where just she and six kids talked about segregation in the city and how they could address and transform the education system for all kids, not just for some. Imxn realized even within the same city, the students desired different things. Imxn wanted cultural representation in her curriculum and teachers who looked like her. Others wanted toilet paper to be consistently provided in their bathrooms, for a start. They chose to build Integrate NYC as an official organization after she graduated, and she's been working with them ever since.

During this conversation, I became curious about how she has continued to stay focused on the communities around her. Many young people see the world's issues as global issues; sometimes it feels as though we should be going everywhere and offering aid. Why keep ourselves in the places we grew up when we could potentially go anywhere and everywhere? But Imxn eloquently offered her perspective on the matter, which put into concrete words what I had come to realize.

"As American kids grow up, the U.S. media always wants us to feel that we're saviors or that we're meant to be saviors of the rest of the world. 'Look at the poor hungry children in Africa,' but there's over 110,000 homeless kids right here in NYC who don't know if they're going to eat either! We tend to forget that the problems that are happening across the world are happening in our own neighborhoods in modern, capitalist ways. I can't focus on other kids being hungry when the kids on my block are being hungry."[167]

"I don't have to go far to change the world," Imxn declared. "Once we heal what's around us, we'll be able to heal the world. If we can't even heal the communities we live in, it will be so much more difficult to connect with people outside of them." As I spoke to Imxn, I recognized this also is a key aspect of resilience—the ability to focus on what we can do versus getting overwhelmed in what we cannot do.

Resilience does not come easy; it will always be easier to give up than to keep fighting. But it is worth being cultivated in anyone, especially the young women of today who want to create a better future for themselves and others. Research on "grit," which is described as the "perseverance and passion for long-term goals," suggests that to achieve difficult goals,

---

167 "On the Map: The Atlas of Student Homelessness in New York City 2017," Institute for Children, Poverty, & Homelessness, August 14, 2017.

one must not only have talent but also apply that talent in a sustained and focused manner over time.[168]

When it comes to being a changemaker, many obstacles will fall into your path. Challenges are unavoidable and, in fact, an essential part of the journey. Without challenges, one would not learn how to acknowledge one's strengths and weaknesses, how to empathize with others, how to be patient, and how to persist even when it seems like you'll never reach your goals. These values create an unshakable leader—the type of leader others will stand behind and want to follow. If you choose one quality to nurture as you start your journey to creating social change, let it be resilience, for it will carry you as far as you dare to go.

---

168 Angela Duckworth et al., "Grit: Perseverance and Passion for Long-Term Goals," *Journal of Personality and Social Psychology* 92, no.6 (2007): 1087-1101.

PART 3

WHAT WE CAN DO

"Remember that no one is born a change-maker. It's something you become when you see a problem, then dare to become part of the solution."

— MELINDA GATES

CHAPTER 8

SHIFT YOUR PERSPECTIVE

———

I remember the first time I wished I was white.

I was in kindergarten, playing with my best friend Annie during recess. I was proudly showing off my slightly faded henna on my tiny palms, a remnant of the wedding I had attended the weekend before. The small flower designs that decorated my hands had me in awe. Even at such a young age, I was enamored with the traditional art. It reminded me of good memories, of an older cousin quickly drawing the design and laughing as I giggled at the way the paste tickled my palm. Annie, also being a young Indian-American girl, was equally mesmerized by it, and we gushed over its beauty excitedly, wondering when we could attend the next wedding.

Suddenly, a few of my white classmates ran over to us, wondering what we were looking at. They looked like a matching set of dolls, with their pale skin, blond hair, and colorful, sequined shirts. Without hesitation, the tallest one pointed at my hands with a dubious expression. "What is *that*?" she drawled, and I proudly displayed my palms to her.

"It's called henna," I said proudly, "and it's one of our traditions at Indian weddings." I smiled brightly, waiting for her to start complimenting the designs the way Annie had.

"Really?" she asked, scrutinizing the patterns. "It looks like dirt to me," she finally declared and then cackled as her friends laughed with her. At a loss for words, I couldn't even respond before she delivered the final blow. "I would never want to put something like that on my hands. Who would want to look like they played in mud?"

With that, she ran off with her little entourage, and I was left fighting tears with Annie frantically trying to console me. When I got home that afternoon, I ran to the bathroom and furiously started scrubbing my palms, wishing the henna would just disappear. *I don't want to be different anymore*, I thought to myself. *I want to be white.* With just one interaction, something I had taken deep pride in suddenly was something to be teased about. It marked me as *other*, and I became ashamed.

Over the years, other interactions made me wish I wasn't Indian, even if it was just for a second. When I was in fourth grade, I watched as every one of my female classmates was invited to a birthday party, except for me. Why, you may ask? The birthday girl thought I wouldn't be able to "connect with them" because—as a brown girl—people assumed I was only interested in school and wouldn't want to spend time doing makeup or talking about boybands. When I was in sixth grade, another friend came to my house for the first time and remarked that she was surprised it didn't "smell like curry."

In my sophomore year of high school, I endured an entire semester of my white male classmate, seated behind me, whispering racial slurs and saying my family members were terrorists. During my senior year of high school, I was on a class field trip in Chicago when a random man started yelling obscenities at me, telling me to "go back to India" and to "stop taking jobs from Americans." In college, I was at a bar when a stranger grabbed me and tried to put his hands all over me. When I pushed him away and told him to stop, he sneered and said, "You should be grateful that anyone even paid attention to an ugly Indian bitch like you."

While, over time, I grew to love and be proud of my heritage, these interactions offer a glimpse of the ways social discrimination can manifest for women, especially women of color. When I spoke up about any type of discrimination, my Indian-American friends would sympathize, but say, "That's just the way it is." If I received respect or an opportunity, I was told to be grateful, "because not all women received the same treatment."

But why is basic respect withheld from women across the world? Why is equal access to opportunity only for the privileged and not considered a right? I'm aware of my privilege, but I don't want these things to be privileges. I want them to be accessible to all women.

It's wonderful to know how essential female empowerment is, but it becomes difficult to decide how to support women.

There are so many ways to enable women and girls to achieve amazing things; it's challenging to decide not only where to start but what to prioritize. With so many organizations, movements, programs, etc., it can feel like there is always a "better" way to help women. However, this only leads to movements stagnating, as no action is being taken. The best way to empower women and girls is to simply start anywhere.

Social empowerment is one of the most powerful forms of support we can provide women. As defined in a 2013 study, it is the "enabling force that strengthens women's social relations and their position in social structures."[169] It emphasizes creating efforts to address social discrimination in society, whether based on race, ethnicity, gender, religion, or disability. Researchers have determined female empowerment is a multi-faceted process, which should inevitably lead to enabling women to realize their full identity and all their powers.[170] Women are often vulnerable to various kinds of exploitation, whether sexual, labor, etc., which makes it even more vital to strengthen their position in society. If this can be achieved, it provides the chance to escape from male domination and assert their equal status with men.[171]

169 Keshab Chandra Mandal, "Concept and Types of Women Empowerment," *International Forum of Teaching and Studies* 9, no. 2 (2013).

170 Valsamma Antony, "Education and Employment: The Key to Women's Empowerment," *Kurukshetra, Journal of Ministry of Rural Development*, 2006.

171 R.S. Srivastava, "Women Empowerment: Some Critical Issue," Abha Avasti and A.K. Srivastava (eds.), *Modernity, Feminism and Women Empowerment*, Rawat Publications, 2001.

It also comes down to helping cultivate a sense of autonomy and self-confidence for women—and this means action on an individual basis and a collective basis to shift social relationships, discourses, and institutions in a way that addresses the disparities between women and men's quality of life.[172]

Women for Women, an organization that invests in vulnerable women throughout the world, socially elevates women by providing resources to help them build the skills, tools, and resources they need to thrive in their communities.[173] They also understand that social empowerment comes from letting women know what their rights are, whether political, economic, or health-wise.[174]

In Nigeria, they have implemented programs that teach women about their land rights, as many women are still deprived of an inheritance that is rightfully theirs. In the Democratic Republic of Congo, they educate the women about protections against gender-based violence. In Bosnia-Herzegovina, young women are trained to be advocates for equality and change within their own communities. The organization also strives to teach women how to take better care of their health and well-being—and that of their

---

172   Emilie Combaz and Claire Mcloughlin, "Social and Economic Empowerment," GSDRC, August 2014.

173   "Our Approach," Women for Women International, accessed June 8, 2020.

174   "Social Empowerment," Women for Women International, accessed June 8, 2020.

families. This can be done through training on nutrition, sanitation, and reproductive rights.[175]

But much of social empowerment comes from addressing the things we see and do every day—the patterns of behaviors and thoughts we don't think to second-guess because they seem "normal" or "natural." Yet when we take a more in-depth look at the elements of society we've normalized, we may find severe issues with what we've deemed acceptable. The direct acts of violence and oppression against women don't always create the greatest challenges; subtle biases also underlie the current of how our societies are run.

REPRESENTATION AND VISIBILITY

Many young women, especially young women of color, grew up in a time where it was very hard to find people who looked like us in popular media. Even the rare chances when we did were often accompanied by some sort of tokenism that attempted to make a single story represent an entire cultural group. In fact, renowned Nigerian author Chimamanda Ngozi Adichie speaks on this topic in one of her most famous TED Talks, "The Danger of a Single Story." She began her presentation by telling a story of her childhood, where she only had access to British and American books that featured "white and blue-eyed" characters. When she started drawing pictures and writing stories of her own, she mimicked what

---

175 Ibid.

she had read; all her characters were white, they played in the snow, and they drank ginger beer.[176]

While it may not seem like a big deal on the surface, Chimamanda expressed what the mimicry really represented. "What this demonstrates," she stated in her speech, "is how impressionable and vulnerable we are in the face of a story, particularly as children." She explained that because all her books had foreign characters, she became convinced that books, "by their very nature," needed to have foreigners and be about things she couldn't personally relate to. However, when she started reading African books, she mentally shifted her view on what literature could be. They helped her realize people such as herself could be featured in stories and saved her from believing a single idea on what books were.[177]

She listed other various examples of a single story—how poverty, catastrophe, media, politics, etc., can dominate our idea of what someone can be. What struck me was her revelation that we cannot talk about these stories without understanding the underlying power dynamics that guide them. "How they are told, who tells them, when they're told, how many stories are told," she emphasized in her speech, "are really dependent on power." Power is not only limited to whether the story of another person is told but also making that one narrative the sole definition of that person.[178]

---

176 Chimamanda Adichie, "The Danger of a Single Story," Filmed July 2009 in Oxford, UK, TED Video. 00:32.

177 Ibid, 1:36.

178 Ibid, 10:04.

When we refuse to account for the multiple stories that make up a person, we rob them of the chance to fully share who they are. We diminish them to one thing because it's easier to place people into small, easily labeled boxes rather than let them hold space across interests and experiences. When I spoke with Litia, the passionate Fijian climate activist, about her experience at her first global conference, she expressed how she went to COP24 with her story on the effects of climate change, and then realized she was being pulled in so many different directions to tell it. After giving four to five interviews some days, she realized halfway through the week that she was being tokenized in that space.

Tokenism is the practice of doing something, like hiring a person from a minority group, only to prevent criticism and give the illusion that people are being treated fairly.[179] "People were using me; as a young brown Pacific Islander woman, I tick off a lot of minority boxes," Litia clarified. "I was warned to be careful about tokenism because some people might say they want to hear your story, but there's not much that they will do with it." Rather than trying to use her story to promote change, they wanted her to become the face of what happened, to show the rest of the world "this is who climate change is having an impact on."

But Litia didn't like being put on the spot and didn't believe her community should be reduced to victims. "I don't think we're victims of climate change, not even colonialism. I refuse to look at us like victims because there's some sort of losing sensation with that word—that means the problem

---

179 *Merriam-Webster*, s.v., "tokenism (n.)," accessed June 8, 2020.

is no longer a problem anymore. But this is a reality we're still facing."

Rather than continue a narrative that paints them as helpless victims, Litia sees her community differently. "I look at us like fighters and warriors. Even if we have small wins now, it's not going to stop us from fighting the larger fight." I couldn't agree more. Her conviction led me to hope that we all stop taking the stories we're told at face value and look deeper to find the actual meaning. When we read a story about a certain person or group of people, I hope we choose to see them for who they really are, not just what the media wanted us to see.

How do we create more representation and visibility for young women? We start by consuming media that demonstrates diverse sets of people. We choose to include books from authors of all backgrounds and stories from all walks of life in our school curriculum. We start demanding our media stop using one single person as a token of an entire demographic but, rather, choose to display multiple perspectives. We need to realize tokenization is not representation in the slightest; it's a subversive tactic to get out of representing a group.

It is also about exposing our young women to other women who are accomplishing things from all walks of life. Whether it be innovative engineers, passionate social justice activists, dedicated physicians, creative artists—young women should be able to see their goals and dreams are valid, and that women before them have done the very same things. We should do our best to not only make ourselves available to talk about our journeys but also to introduce them to a diverse set of potential role models, whether through our personal connections, documentaries, or looking through the internet.

For example, A Mighty Girl is a website filled with books, television shows, movies, toys, and other resources to help raise "smart, confident, and courageous girls." It even has a weekly newsletter parents can sign up for to introduce their young daughters to trailblazing women and girls from across the world—almost like a bite-size version of this book! These empowering resources teach them they don't have to just be the damsel in distress. They can be the leaders and heroes in their own stories as well.180 The younger you start widening their heuristic of what a woman can be, the more likely they can grow with confidence. As a bottom line, help them be aware of who they can be by providing them a variety of examples to look to.

THE BEAUTY OF BEING MULTI-DIMENSIONAL

In the fall of 2019, I took a political analysis course taught by Dr. Deondra Rose. Now, if you're familiar with Duke's Public Policy department, you'll know that Professor Rose is one of the most adored faculty members our university has to offer. My fellow students (and even TAs!) often joked about how when Dr. Rose entered the classroom, she didn't walk down the stairs; she floated. She exudes radiance. She's beyond intelligent, incredibly accomplished, and effortlessly friendly. One might even say she's not-so-secretly everyone's idol.

---

180 "About," A Mighty Girl, accessed June 8, 2020.

When I interviewed her for *Rise*, I was incredibly excited to highlight her but didn't expect to find any common ground. I thought I would merely ask a few questions, jot down some answers, and then bid her goodbye.

But what was intended to be a twenty-minute conversation lasted well over an hour. And the funniest thing is we found out we both shared the most niche experience, having done pageants when we were younger. I began by asking about her experiences as an academic and her journey to where she is now.

"I've always been very confident and comfortable in my skin. But I found as I started to move into different professional arenas, as a grad student in particular, there were some moments where people would really practice judging my former self," she explained as I diligently took notes. "I'm an academic, I'm a professor, I'm a researcher, I'm a scholar; being an academic is a serious profession and it is important work! As a scholarship student, when I was in college, I used to do pageants and..."

"Wait a minute," I interrupted, my hands hovering over my keyboard. "You did pageants too?" *It all makes sense now*, I thought to myself. The poise, the presence, *her power.* "That's so crazy because I did a few when I was younger too!" I shared excitedly, and we both laughed and immediately started talking about our experiences. We lamented about the issues of diversity, and the unevenness in representation. After all, we had been among the few women of color who'd participated in each event.

"As someone who was self-financing higher education through scholarships and work," she resumed, "part of my interest in the pageant was that it was also a—"

"*Scholarship opportunity!*" we both said in unison. I couldn't believe it; it was like she was speaking about my own life. "Did you ever have people give you a weird reaction when you talked about how you had done pageants in the past?" I inquired. I don't often bring up the fact that I did a few pageants in the past because it often is met with strange looks and disbelief. *You did pageants, Shana? That's not like you at all.* While I may not have initially wanted to take part in the pageants, I can't help but feel irked by that appraisal. All I can ever think in response is, *Well, what's THAT supposed to mean?*

"Yes, I can definitely think of at least one memory about that," she stressed. "I remember sitting in one of my classes in grad school, and somehow it came up that I had done scholarship pageants in the past. A classmate then looked at me HORRIFIED, saying, 'You did pageants?' When I told her that I had, she responded with absolute disgust."

I nodded in empathy because I'd also witnessed similar reactions. We both could relate that it can be hard for women to feel we can express different sides of ourselves, or even talk about the things we did in the past to get to where we are. "I feel like as I was growing up, I would hide parts of myself because it didn't fit people's images of who I was," I responded. "Pageants are one thing, but growing up, I felt that people couldn't reconcile that I could be really interested in other things apart from just caring about school as a person of Indian descent." I mean, how often have we seen the "Indian nerd" stereotype played out in the media in the past? And how often did they ever have fashionable outfits or participate in clubs that weren't academically oriented? How often were they the stars of their gym class?

"For example, when I said I was really passionate about dance," I continued, "people would automatically dismiss it, thinking I either wasn't actually that good at dancing or believing I should drop it to focus more on school. I was on the dance team all three years in middle school and most people didn't even notice me until my final year. I literally dressed up for every game! Like, come on!" I huffed exasperatedly, and I could almost hear Dr. Rose's empathetic smile on the other side of the line.

"I totally understand. At the time, I felt a little embarrassed because grad school is socially challenging. We have so many reasons to feel embarrassed, but I made a promise that I would always advocate for my previous self," she declared. "I would always respect the person I had been because those phases and iterations of me have contributed to the person I am."

"Yeah I did 'pageants,'" she continued, "and I enjoyed it and I met some of my best friends. I had some of my greatest experiences and learned some of the best lessons that I can apply to other situations." She emphasized we should never let people make us feel self-conscious about our journeys.

It's very easy to throw stereotypes and judge each other. But one thing I learned from my conversation with Dr. Rose was that, in most cases, it doesn't matter what people think. We should aim to liberate ourselves from other people's judgments and recognize the value in every opportunity. Rather than hide your experiences, use them as a testament to your capacity to learn from different viewpoints, walks of life, and social circles. Some people think it's intimidating rather than interesting for a woman to wear so many hats, but that's what makes humanity diverse and allows connection past the surface.

If we seek to empower women, it starts with recognizing their ability to be multi-dimensional human beings. Their power does not come from catering to the image we force upon them; it comes from their freedom to embrace every part of themselves equally.

PREJUDICES AND BIASES

If we're talking about social empowerment, we can't ignore one of the greatest contributors to the oppression of women of color across the world: institutionalized prejudices and biases. Women of color, especially Black and brown women, often struggle the most against the systems created to keep them down and away from equal opportunities and respect.

In fact, many health disparities demonstrate women of color typically face worse health outcomes than their white counterparts. For example, in 2011, researchers at Washington University in St. Louis surveyed 2,500 women aged fourteen to forty-five in a cohort study regarding barriers to contraceptive use. They found women of color, specifically African-American women, had increased odds of using less effective contraceptive methods due to discrimination.181 There were also discrepancies in the rates of unintended pregnancies and lack of contraception use among women of color when compared to their white counterparts. The study aimed to show that when women of color encounter racism and discrimination from health care providers, it impacts their ability to get the care they not only need but deserve.

This is just one study that demonstrates this type of outcome, but hundreds more illustrate similar negative consequences for women of color. If this type of discrimination prevents women of color from accessing health resources, which many of us would hope to be distributed based on need, in how many other areas of life do these biases affect them?

The answer is, unfortunately, all the areas, especially in societies like the United States. Whether it be higher incarceration rates, residential segregation, or less access to quality education, women of color are constantly battling for a spot on an even playing field in the game of life.182 Their concerns range from financial security to protecting the lives of their families, because this type of discrimination can escalate to the point of violence and even the death of innocents.

As a first-generation Indian American, I straddle the line between being a person of color who may face discrimination

---

181 Karla Kossler et al., "Perceived Racial, Socioeconomic and Gender Discrimination and Its Impact on Contraceptive Choice," *Contraception* 84, no. 3 (2011): 273-9.

182 "Discrimination," Office of Disease Prevention and Health Promotion, accessed June 8, 2020.

to an extent and benefiting from immense privileges. South Asian culture, unfortunately, does have racial biases that affect the behavior and mentalities of many.

Many believe false narratives about other minority groups, such as that they are not motivated or don't have strong family values.[183] They may subscribe to the notion that if you simply work hard and have the drive, you will succeed, an idea that directly comes from the "model minority" myth. South Asian Americans (and the larger Asian American population in general) look to their own struggles, their own pain, and wonder why other minorities, such as Black people, can't succeed if they were able to.

But while Asian Americans may face discrimination, they haven't gone through the systemic dehumanization Black people have faced in America through slavery and the continued oppression.[184] Not just Asian Americans need to change, but everyone in positions of privilege.

We can't continue to stay silent in addressing racial disparities because it's a matter of people's lives. For those of us not directly affected by racial injustices every day, it can be an uncomfortable topic of conversation or, at the very least, make us defensive or feel guilty.

---

183 Kat Chow, "'Model Minority' Myth Again Used as A Racial Wedge Between Asians And Blacks," *NPR*, April 19, 2017.

184 Claire Jean Kim, "Model Minority' Myth Again Used as A Racial Wedge Between Asians And Blacks," interviewed by Kat Chow, NPR, April 19, 2017.

But these feelings won't lead to productive conversations or enacting change. It starts by acknowledging another person's suffering does not invalidate your own struggles or hardship. Rather, if we have overcome our own obstacles, why not support those in need? Why not fight for our society to value the lives of other people, regardless of whether they are different from us? At the very least, we must stop generalizing the narratives that attribute negative traits to an entire population.

While most of the people in my life may not be racist, many of them aren't actively anti-racist. I used to think not being racist was enough, that not harming anyone or participating in such acts was all I needed to do as an ally. But as I've tried to further educate myself on racial tensions and disparities, I've found neutrality isn't enough. We can have as many good intentions as we want, but at the end of the day, action is required to create the needed paradigm shifts. If we're not at least trying to help, or choose to remain silent, we're giving more power to the oppressor rather than the oppressed.

I understand it may be intimidating to face the issue head on, but you're in a position of privilege if you've avoided participating in these conversations and efforts up until now. Rather than be ashamed of your privilege, use it to amplify the voices of those being silenced.

Look within and confront your own implicit biases. Where did they come from? How did your concepts of privilege, sexism, racism, etc., affect your upbringing? How do you continue to benefit from systems that cause others to suffer, and what can you do to dismantle those systems?

Don't be afraid to call out discriminatory behavior and/or comments; it holds people accountable and forces important conversations. Listen to educators who belong to the minority groups affected, and refrain from the desire to insert your own thoughts/ideas/opinions unless asked. If you do have access to relevant resources, do your own research rather than putting the burden on the groups being oppressed to educate you.

Don't be reluctant to have these conversations outside of your family/friend circles too. Having them in your workplace, academic settings, and more will apply the pressure needed for change to happen. Implement mandatory anti-racist and anti-bias training. Create zero-tolerance policies. Pressure our government systems to condemn such behavior within their own ranks, and to enact the appropriate consequences if such actions arise. If we fight on all fronts, we have a chance at dismantling the biases and behaviors that put down people of color, and especially women of color.

From what I've seen, prejudices and biases are the underlying causes of many of our global issues today. Social structures have been created to keep women from not only being recognized for their accomplishments and skills but also from receiving the support and resources necessary to take complete ownership over their own lives. We need to start by examining our own behaviors and thought patterns, taking stock of the biases we may possess and actively trying to dismantle them. Harmful biases extend far past race; make sure to confront other examples such as homophobia, xenophobia, ageism, classism, religious prejudice, and more.

Social empowerment also comes from celebrating our young women, reminding them of their value and the inherent rights they deserve. Regardless of the biases other people may possess, let them know they are people too. They shouldn't be treated as objects, they shouldn't stand for people discriminating against them, and they should understand their thoughts, ideas, and contributions matter. They should be respected physically, emotionally, socially, and mentally. They should confidently believe they are more than just their race, gender, social status, etc. They are a combination of their talents, dreams, values, and everything else that makes them who they are.

If you're struggling to find ways to emphasize these qualities, organizations such as the Girls Empowerment Network seek to empower young girls by giving them the skills to thrive and encourage them to believe in their own power.[185] Through workshops, community involvement, and other methods, these organizations exemplify the roles we all have to play in helping young girls and women improve their self-efficacy. Look for ways to bring these resources within your own homes and communities because all of us need to play a part.

For social empowerment to occur, let us remember it's not only the young women who need to believe they deserve these rights, opportunities, and recognition. We all need to believe it as well and act accordingly to create a new reality for them.

---

185 "About Us," Girls Empowerment Network, accessed June 8, 2020.

CHAPTER 9

START 'EM YOUNG

———

You close your eyes as the smell of saltwater embraces you like an old friend. When you open them, you wonder at the mosaic of colors that paint the sky; you could swear you've never seen such vibrant shades of orange, pink, and yellow in your life. You choose to walk along the shore, feet sinking in the soft sand beneath as you watch the tide come forward and rush back. It's the first moment in a while where you've felt so at peace. When was the last time you slowed down like this? When was the last time you hadn't hoped for the seconds to tick so you could move onto the next thing?

As you continue down the shoreline, you notice two young girls skipping together ahead of you. They play together, laughing and jumping in the waves without a care in the world. They shriek as the ocean teases their toes and run after it as it recedes. They don't think logically about the fact that the tide will return, or maybe they just don't care due to the thrill of the chase. Their smiles seem to compete with the sinking sun—in your eyes, they're shining even brighter than it.

You look at them, wondering what happened to you as you grew older. Here are these young girls, so locked in the moment and overflowing with joy. But as you watch them, you can't help but feel the complete opposite: lost, confused, and downhearted. Had you always been like this or had life just made you feel this way?

This isn't a random daydream, but a prominent memory from the life of Melody Pourmoradi, the creator of The GiRLiFE Empowerment Series. When I participated in her online workshop, she recounted this moment from a past vacation as one of the main motivations for creating a girls' empowerment program. As she watched her daughters live in the present that day, she realized women faced a huge disconnect from childhood to their adulthood. She reflected on her own life, on how her parents had spoken to her a child—the things she used to hear from her well-meaning parents, the messaging that had the most beautiful intentions, communicated with what they knew at the time.

"I was taught to dim my light, turn down the volume on my voice, to hold it in," she revealed to me when we spoke. She described how when she was younger, she may have felt some confidence, but she then struggled for years. "There are certain ideals that influence the way we want to be seen, especially in the media, on what a typical girl should feel, look like, act like, etcetera. I felt that I didn't fit in with any of these ideals, which lowered my self-esteem."

While she eventually grew out of this mentality that she wasn't "good enough," she knew there had to be a way to prevent more girls from suffering a similar fate. After reflecting on the support she could've benefited from as a young girl, she wanted to create a curriculum and certification program to dismantle the limitations, stereotypes, and expectations that hinder a girl's ability to flourish as an adult. Thus, GiR-LiFE Empowerment was born.

When I learned about the program, I was so in awe. Melody's struggle with self-confidence is an obstacle many young women face, and one I know well. I can think of countless times when I've felt like I wasn't "enough," when I never saw people who looked like me in the media, when I didn't do well on an assignment, when I was convinced my worth was solely determined by external recognition and validation. And through it all, I believed every person just had to suffer through it. It eventually had to get better, right?

But had I been in a program like GiRLiFE, maybe I could have avoided all the tears and anxiety, or at least lessen the presence of those negative emotions in my life. I can clearly remember the days in elementary school when I used to wish I wasn't a girl. *If I were a boy, life would be so much easier,* I thought. No one would say things about what I wore or tell me I should be quieter. I wouldn't have to worry about being "pretty enough." People wouldn't expect me to smile and be nice all the time!

As I got older, my inner conversation became more self-degrading. *I'm not smart enough, I'm not good enough. I'm too quiet, I'm too loud. Why can't I just look like her? Why can't I just be like her? If I were more* [insert unattainable quality here], *people would like me more, or things would work out better.*

If I didn't want the weird looks and wolf whistles, maybe I shouldn't have worn that outfit. Was it my fault? But I didn't want attention...or did I? Am I just an attention-seeker? I should have dressed more modestly...who do I even think I am? What did I expect?

Maybe my ideas were dumb, or I was talking too much; I probably deserved to be interrupted. I should just shut up and give up. Why am I even trying anymore? I can't accomplish those huge, crazy dreams. I'm not meant for those things.

If we only decide to start empowering young women when they are old enough to understand the injustices they face, we're too late. Female empowerment isn't always about the environment outside; a woman must internally understand what it means to be empowered as well. This is where female psychological empowerment comes to play, which can be defined as "a blend of self-esteem, self-efficacy, self-determination, self-confidence, self-awareness, positive thinking, and it ultimately leads to well-being and happiness of women."[186]

It is essential to begin cultivating these qualities and this confidence from a young age, as the qualities encouraged as a child tend to affect a person over their lifetime.[187] In this case, the parents, guardians, relatives, and other development

186 Gunjan Mishra, "The Psychological Facets of Women Empowerment at Workplace," *International Journal of Recent Trends in Engineering & Research* 2, no. 11 (2016).

187 Christopher J. Mruk, *Self-Esteem and Positive Psychology, 4th Edition* (New York; Springer, 2013).

supporters need to take responsibility in consciously making an effort to help girls understand, throughout their lives, that being a female doesn't mean automatic limitations on what they can and cannot do. It's about encouraging them to be whoever they want to be, regardless of what societal expectations wish to hold them down.

Gender socialization is a type of primary socialization in which children learn what it means to be male or female, usually using their parents or adults as guides. People will attempt to assign genders to certain traits—qualities such as sensitivity, kindness, and sympathy are considered feminine, while independence, boldness, and self-confidence are considered masculine. Depending on what children witness, they learn what is considered "normal" and generally adopt the behaviors most associated with social approval.[188]

If we tolerate certain traits only when displayed by a specific gender, we are doing a disservice to all people. There should be freedom to express one's personality without social penalties, and good qualities shouldn't be limited based on gender expectations. Boys should be encouraged to be kind and sympathetic, while girls should find their independence and self-confidence are valued, no matter their stage of development.

A commonality among development studies is that girls are often encouraged and praised differently than boys are. A long-term study demonstrated that even though parents

188   Neil Moonie, *GCE AS Level Health and Social Care Single Award Book (For OCR)*, (Oxford: Heinemann, 2005), 5.

praised both genders equally, boys were praised for their efforts 24.4 percent of the time; girls were only praised in the same manner 10.3 percent of the time.[189] Rather than being praised for having certain qualities, boys are more often praised for what they do with those qualities. The difference results in boys more often believing they can build upon their strengths and skills, while girls often believe they can't develop the traits they already possess.

What would happen if we simply started encouraging and praising girls for making an effort? What if we started allowing girls to roughhouse and play, to be loud and talkative the way boys can? At the very least, it would stop perpetuating the imbalance of self-efficacy and self-confidence developed between the genders.

As I took the online course with Melody, I noticed how her daughters, now in their teens, were supporting the class energetically by commenting and liking messages almost instantaneously. When I interviewed Melody, I asked if she saw a difference in the way she grew up from the way she was raising her daughters. Rather than elaborate on the important role she must have taken in their lives, she caught me off guard with her candid response. "My daughters are my greatest teachers," she told me. "I've had a lot of the growth in the past few years, and it's all through them. I'm learning from them and also guiding them."

189 Lindsay Abrams, "Study: Praise Children for What They Do, Not Who They Are," *The Atlantic,* February 12, 2013.

"But how exactly do you guide them? What do you say?" I asked eagerly. After all, I was looking for concrete steps and actions to take. From what I've learned, good intentions can only go so far and often miss the mark without the proper techniques and methods to communicate them.

"The messaging in our home is that you have so much power within you, and when you know about that power, you can use that power," she revealed. "So many girls walk around not knowing their power, but you have a million and one powers that come in the form of talents and strengths." She's come to adore the fact that her daughters live out every passion and dream. They'll give anything a shot, and they won't back down from the challenge on their heart. When Melody was younger and confronted with a challenge, she would say, "I can't do that." In contrast, her daughters think, "Who am I not to do that?"

The way others talk to a young woman holds great influence on the way she talks to herself. Your idea of how resilient you are, how intelligent and capable you are, etc., often stems from the views the people around you possessed and shared with you. These ideas are reinforced based on what is praised or what is admonished, and the social approval associated with certain qualities over others. Dr. Heidi Grant Halvorson, associate director of the Motivation Science Center and Columbia Business School, and director of the Diversity & Bias Practice at the NeuroLeadership Institute, found that "girls who develop self-control earlier and can better follow instructions are often praised for their 'goodness.'" As they continue to get praised on qualities they believe are innate and unchangeable, they evolve into women who will "prematurely conclude that they don't have what it takes to succeed in a particular arena and give up way too soon.[190]

If we only praise girls for quietly following directions, how will they learn to use their voices and vocalize their disagreement? How will they learn to advocate for themselves and for others, to question the unfair expectations they face, to continue on when the situation seems bleak?

This is why the word "disruptor" has become popular in media today—and it refers to all the women taking a stance and challenging what society expects of them. People like Victory Jones and Tori Elizabeth, founders of The Colored Girl, have created a company that unites and represents women of color throughout the globe. As explained in an interview with Authority Magazine, they believe "we all deserve the same opportunities, to [be] represented fairly and treated equally." Their company received global attention after being featured by Essence Magazine, and they are the epitome of women who have become psychologically empowered enough to realize what they deserve and have found ways to fight for a better and more inclusive world.[191]

When I spoke to Andrea Alejandra Gonzales about her journey as an activist against gun violence, she mentioned her father was a huge influence on her current lifestyle. As an

190   Heidi Grant Halvorson, "The Trouble with Bright Girls," *Psychology Today*, January 27, 2011.

191   Erika Ashley, "Female Disruptors: The Colored Girl Is Empowering Women of Color to Thrive," *Authority Magazine*, Medium, October 9, 2018.

activist himself, her father had never shied away from tough conversations on global issues. Andrea recalled one of her earliest memories from when she was about five years old, having a long conversation with her father about the wars in Iraq and Afghanistan. To my surprise, she detailed how he even went into the social and economic issues that contributed to the conflict, despite her young age.

While some adults may have excluded such complicated subjects from a conversation with a child, he took the time to explain them to her because he felt she needed to know. "I remember that moment so vividly," she told me. "I learned about who really is our community and who is advocating for what we believe in. I learned that what we believe in often comes from people in power, even if they don't know what's up."

Her father's effortless balance of masculine and feminine energy was inspiring to Andrea. Many of the males she encountered in her life have been very hostile, communicating with random violent outbursts filled with harsh words. She recognized these outbursts were not always intentional, that they were a defense mechanism people are often taught. For many, it's a show of power, and they're told they need to do this to feel safe or heard.

"My dad was able to get rid of that defense, showing that he could be kind and vulnerable in his words," she described fondly. As a result, she learned to be at peace with herself and others; her father had rooted himself within that, learning to be protective and soft, being open-minded and strong in his ideas, and being balanced at all times.

When I asked Andrea how it felt to be encouraged in such a positive way from a young age, she couldn't speak more highly of the experience. "I absolutely loved it," she declared. "I would go out into the world and I'd experience certain types of violence at school or in the community; I'd be really fragile about that but come home and be reminded of the kindness that does exist, that violence and hate is not inherent but it's something we need to unlearn."

She learned she could get through life being kind, that it's been done before. Her dad was a passionate activist and did it by being a kind, loving, and joyful human. With his encouragement and positive influence, Andrea discovered an inner confidence that allowed her to continue her path of activism, even in the face of harm and difficulty.

Andrea's story illustrates the power of encouraging young women at a young age. Not everyone may share the same values of radical love and kindness that Andrea holds in high esteem, but we should seek to learn her commitment to them. She does not balk in the face of a challenge but rather acknowledges the obstacles and knows she can continue to lead in a way that is true to her nature. She's learned to be rooted in her principles and to never conform to what other people want her to be. With such strong messaging and role models guiding her, she's chased her dreams and accomplished her goals without compromising the most important parts of herself.

So when does psychological empowerment start? Ideally, from the moment they're born. If we can raise young women to have high self-esteem, it only will help them take on the challenges they will inevitably face. It's been found that high self-esteem leads to an increased sense of competence, which encourages people to risk failure for a chance at success, as they believe they can handle the potential loss or setback.[192] If cultivated in young women, they'll aim higher from the start and give their best efforts. They will recognize their self-worth and take control of their lives, taking ownership of their bodies and income. It will give them the mental strength needed to become tough and hardworking.

When psychologically empowered, women not only will transform themselves but also transgress traditional and patriarchal taboos, analyze social obligations, and question the validity of the expectations they face. They will be more willing to take risks, and it will increase their likelihood of joining educational institutions, political parties, and other decision-making bodies, where their opinions and ideas will lead to a tsunami of positive changes being implemented as their voices and experiences start to be included.[193]

Encouraging women to join any institution and occupation gives them opportunities to see and to know more of the world than those who have been stuck in the household against their will. They will learn how to better adapt to changing circumstances and find better life satisfaction. When we look at the benefits of encouraging young women

---

192   Mruk, *Self Esteem and Positive Psychology.*

193   Zara Mallam Musa et al., "Psychological Empowerment and Engagement in Income-Generating Activities among Rural Women in Yobe State, Nigeria," *IOSR Journal of Humanities And Social Science* 22, no.10 (2016):70-84.

from the start, there is no denying the impact our words and minds have on the potential of our society.

If we want to lift up our young women, we need to acknowledge the power our presence has on them. It's essential to deliver the message to our young people that the people we spend time with are the people we become. We need to remind them of their unique talents. We must demonstrate our unwavering support by showing up consistently, during the times of celebration and the times when they're knocked down. We should be reflecting on our own lives and how we could serve as an example of the type of people they can be. Above all, we need to remember we have a part to play in building the mental strength they need to achieve the incredible feats that will positively impact our world.

CHAPTER 10

LET THEM LIVE AND LEARN

———

It was a beautiful day in late August, sunny without a cloud in the sky, the temperature at a perfect 75 degrees Fahrenheit with a gentle breeze providing cool relief every so often. In fact, there couldn't have been a more perfect day to welcome me onto Duke University's campus for the first time. Young students walked with their families, laughing and chattering excitedly about the coming school year and the memories they would make. Exuberant campus ambassadors proudly relayed the history of this prestigious institution, and as I passed in front of the Duke chapel, a cute elderly couple wearing matching Duke t-shirts took a selfie with the brightest smiles. It was like I had walked right into a college admission commercial. But as I stared up at the majestic chapel that stood proudly in the center of campus, only one thought came to mind.

God, I'm doomed.

For the first time in my life, I was in an academic setting I felt incredibly overwhelmed by. Even though students were smiling, laughing, and talking as they passed by me, it was about some quantum physics joke I still don't think I would understand even if it was explained to me. When a family came near me, the parents were reminiscing about their own experiences at Duke and how they couldn't wait for their kids to have the same ones. Meanwhile, I was WhatsApping my dad photos of the tall trees because he said he wanted to compare North Carolina's greenery to Kerala's, as he'd never even visited the state. I thought I would catch a break with the campus ambassador, but I should've known better than to ask him what he did over the summer. "Oh! I went to Seychelles with some friends after spending two months in Vietnam teaching kids English," he responded brightly. "What did you do?" *Who are you, Michelle Obama?* I thought incredulously.

"Oh, you know, just a retail job and spending some time with family at home," I responded weakly. It took every ounce of self-control to not run back to my hometown screaming. I had come to Duke believing I would feel like I was meant to be here. I had to be qualified if I was standing here as a transfer student, right? But suddenly, the quality of education I had been so excited by felt above my capacity. Was I even on par with any of these students if I couldn't find any common ground with them on the first day? I overestimated myself, *clearly.*

But before I could spiral into despair and book my immediate return flight to O'Hare, I got a reminder on my phone. "Ammachi's birthday! Send up a prayer for her!" the message chimed. I looked at my phone background as I swiped the alert away, gazing at my smiling grandmother's face. My grandma had passed away during my senior year of high school, but I still thought about her constantly. I thought back to working on my homework at my cousins' house when I was in middle and high school.

Every night I was over there working, she'd always hobble over to us and just watch us work with a small smile on her face. "Did you know that before I was pulled out of school, I was first in my class in the fourth grade! I was the best, so everyone would always ask to look at my slate for the answers!" she'd cackle. Back then, my grandmother was pulled out of school after fourth grade, because during her childhood it was considered too expensive to send girls to school. Her father didn't recognize the value her education could've brought her and her family. A few years later, she had an arranged marriage to my grandfather in her teen years, and she continued to be a farmer and housewife for the rest of her life.

One of her greatest regrets was not being able to study past that year, which she'd often express sadly when she watched us work on our homework. But watching her children and grandchildren, and especially her granddaughters, work so diligently brought her a lot of joy. She'd always tell me, "Shana, keep studying hard! Do great things!" I'd always smile at her and resume my studying without much thought, but always a little happier to think I was making her proud.

After getting that message, I could imagine my grandma chastising me from the afterlife. *Shana, don't you dare get*

scared. What did I tell you about focusing on your studies!
The people around me probably thought I was crazy, but I couldn't help but laugh out loud at the thought of my grandmother waving her cane threateningly at me from the heavens. I had always loved school and learning, but I also worked hard to fulfill the dreams my grandparents and family had for me too. If I ran away from an opportunity for a better education now, what was the point of working all this time to have this chance? I sighed, shot up a quick prayer and *"my bad, happy birthday!"* to my grandma, and walked toward my dorm to unpack my things and settle into my new life at Duke.

For many of us, going to school every weekday was a given; it's a basic right and a normalized part of life. After all, about 135 countries have made constitutional provisions for free and non-discriminatory education for all people.[194] But even with these provisions, 132 million girls worldwide still are not in school, and equality continues to be a struggle.[195] Unfortunately, only 66 percent of countries have achieved gender parity in primary education, and the percentage tends to diminish for many countries as the level of education increases.[196] While many factors contribute to this crisis, such as location, war conflict, poverty, etc., cultural stigma and negative stereotypes are common barriers to female education.

---

194 UNESCO, "2010 Education for All Global Monitoring Report — Reaching the Marginalized," accessed June 8, 2020.

195 "Not Educating Girls Costs Countries Trillions of Dollars, Says New World Bank Report," The World Bank, July 11, 2018.

196 "Global Education Monitoring Report," UNESCO, accessed June 8, 2020.

The marginalization of girls' potential comes from years of gender stereotypes across cultures. Misconceptions are used to validate this lack of education access—beliefs that girls are weak at reasoning, should be married off early as their sole duty is to procreate, or are a burden to the family. And it's considered gracious that they even were allowed to live in countries where female feticide is still legal.[197] While people may believe refraining from putting girls in schools will help communities continue on to social and economic glory, the opposite is true.

In reality, the longer girls are in school, the less likely they'll be married off early or become pregnant as teenagers. This would reduce maternal mortality rates and infant mortality rates significantly, as the incidence of these rates is more prevalent among teenage expectant mothers.[198]

Investing in education for girls means millions of dollars are saved from having to address these medical complications alone. Other medical complications for their family members and future children also can be avoided if they're better educated as well, saving even more money in the long run. Also, by educating young women, who are now likely healthier since they're continuing school, millions of jobs can now be performed. Think about it—if 50 percent of a society's population is not allowed to perform compensated work, a huge sector of potential economic benefits isn't being tapped into.

---

197 Julius Kirya, "Women's Empowerment: The Key to Social and Economic Development," Global Health Corps, March 31, 2015.

198 "Maternal Mortality," World Health Organization, September 19, 2019.

While I may have grown up with the privilege of having education considered an indisputable right within my own family, I'm aware of stories from across the world of girls struggling to have the same opportunities. To look deeper into a different perspective, I reached out to Nabila Abbas, a young rural development and education activist from Pakistan. When I connected with her through Skype, I immediately noticed her gentle and confident demeanor. Even though she apologized for the potential difficulty in communication, as English isn't her first language, I had more trouble communicating in English than she did! As we conversed, Nabila offered me an inside look at her own story.

"I was born in a very dismal area in rural Pakistan. I was the sixth child, and being a daughter, people would consider me not as beneficial compared to a boy," she narrated, and I nodded my head in agreement. This type of mentality is unfortunately still present in many communities across the world, and it pains me that it perpetuates when girls have so much to offer our world. However, Nabila assured me her upbringing was different.

"My parents raised me really well, and they gave me opportunities for equal education and basic rights. Since I was born in a rural area, we didn't have equal opportunities for basic rights like education and a strong health system." Nabila considered herself a natural activist, as in her childhood, she wanted to join sports, but in rural areas, girls weren't allowed to participate.

However, she pushed against this stereotype and insisted they let her join. She eventually played on a national level, which started letting the community allow girls to participate. As she grew older, she knew she wanted to further educate herself, setting her sights on aviation management in the urban city of Lahore. While initially met with resistance, she held over a dozen meetings with her parents in which she established that she would pursue this career and wanted their support.

But even when she got her family's support, Nabila recalled a distinctive moment that propelled her to where she is today. It was the morning of her university program interview, and her family did not have the money available for the bus fare to the city. Her mother, who initially was most against the idea, ended up rushing to fellow community members to borrow money so Nabila wouldn't miss this chance. Throughout the entire bus ride, Nabila was dreaming and thinking about how her interview could go. What would the buildings be like? What questions would they ask in her interview? What could this chance mean for her future?

As Nabila walked into the building where her interview was to take place, she suddenly found herself feeling out of place. All around her were girls from the city with glamorous outfits and obvious displays of wealth, and then there was Nabila, a rural tribal girl who had struggled to find the bus fare to get to the university in the first place. But rather than fold into herself and let insecurity take over, Nabila promised herself one thing. *No matter how empty in pocket I am right now, I am full of passion, which I can use as a tool.*

When she came face to face with the director of her department, she launched into a passionate description of her dreams, advocating for herself and her goals without hesitation. To her surprise, the director stood up and gave her a standing ovation at the end of her speech. "Nabila," he said, "you are the one girl out of the many we have interviewed who has touched our hearts with your passion. You have a strong vision to pursue this degree in this department, so we will strongly endorse and recommend you. We will wholeheartedly support you throughout your journey here." Nabila couldn't believe it, but she was granted a full scholarship based on this opportunity to demonstrate her passion, dedication, and determination.

With the chance to pursue higher education, she started various organizations such as the Aviation Forum, where current students help rural girls navigate both financial and social issues with getting an education. They grew from initially serving ten to fifteen people to five hundred people, later including both girls and boys. Nabila's life had inspired several key questions that directed her focus. If rural communities don't have access to education, how are they supposed to learn about the issues they face? How are they supposed to advocate for themselves? She started her activist life in sports but now is devoted to equal opportunities for education and equal rights for rural areas.

Since this day, Nabila has gone on to represent Pakistan to hundreds of delegates around the globe in discussions on education and rural development. She now works with National Youth for Pakistan, which seeks to develop student defenders to protect the rights of women and girls at school and in the workplace to protect them against sexual harassment and other issues. Nabila is a role model for many young people and demonstrates the power an education can provide a young girl, and how she will use that education to empower others as well.

As the Global Health Corps puts it, "The education of girls is equivalent to the education of a nation." Education doesn't merely improve health for girls themselves; according to the World Bank, its positive impact spreads out to other aspects of life and other people as well.[199] When we promote girls' education, we educate more than just the young female students; we educate their friends, their current families, their future families, and their communities. Women who have secondary education tend to have better decision-making abilities within their household, especially regarding their own health care. Their children are less likely to be malnourished, more likely to go to school, and are usually healthier.[200] These women are also likely to experience less intimate partner violence and higher levels of psychological well-being.[201] In sum, better education for girls allows them to participate as full and active members in their communities and society overall.

---

199 "Not Educating Girls Costs Countries Trillions of Dollars," The World Bank.

200 Umme K. Khattak, Saima P. Iqbal, and Haider Ghazanfar, "The Role of Parents' Literacy in Malnutrition of Children Under the Age of Five Years in a Semi-Urban Community of Pakistan: A Case-Control Study," *Cureus* 9, no. 6 (2017).

201 Agumasie Semahegn et al., "Are Interventions Focused on Gender-Norms Effective in Preventing Domestic Violence against Women in Low and Lower-Middle Income Countries? A Systematic Review and Meta-Analysis," *Reproductive Health* 16, no. 93 (2019).

Access to higher levels of education allows girls to have the chance to change their lives and the lives of others. The world benefits from educating more young women. A young girl could be hiding the cure for cancer, the solution to climate change, or a new technological innovation that could benefit millions, but without education, it's way more difficult to have these come to light.

The efforts to stop negative cultural norms from diminishing their potential are important. Free and compulsory education for young women helps them be aware of their rights and possible resources they can use to help them fight to improve their quality of life. As researcher P.H. Sethumadhava Rao states, "an educated mother is a one thousand fold superior to a mere lecturer."[202] While not all young women may choose to be mothers in the future, it's imperative to understand they will help raise the next generation of children and that their potential influence is very powerful. A study conducted in Nairobi found the mother's education persisted as a strong predictor of a child's nutritional status in urban slum settings, even after controlling for other potential factors. It went on to suggest an emphasis on girl-child education was the key to breaking the poverty cycle and improving health outcomes.[203]

---

202 P.H. Sethumadhava Rao, "Education for Women's Empowerment," Promilla Kapur (ed.), *Empowering the Indian Women,* Ministry of Information and Broadcasting, Government of India, New Delhi 2001.

203 Benta A. Abuya, James Ciera, and Elizabeth Kimani-Murage, "Effect of Mother's Education on Child's Nutritional Status in the Slums of Nairobi," *BMC Pediatrics* 12, no. 80 (2012).

Educating girls and young women is also the key to saving the global economy trillions of dollars. In 2018, World Bank reports estimated a loss of about $15 to $30 trillion in lifetime earnings due to the number of girls still out of school.[204] While some may cite an economic loss for putting funds toward girls' education, the benefits far outweigh the costs. According to the Organization for Economic Cooperation and Development (OECD), a report on gender equality within education, entrepreneurship, and employment discovered "increased education accounts for about half of economic growth in [the thirty-four] OECD countries in the past fifty years, and that has a lot to do with bringing more girls to higher levels of education and achieving greater equality in the number of years spent in education between men and women."[205]

Education doesn't have to be limited to normal school subjects either. Health education programs are some of the most powerful initiatives that can be implemented both inside and outside the classroom. For example, teaching women and their surrounding community members about the benefits of family planning and birth control, along with providing access to these services, allows societies to become healthier and economically flourish.

On the Netflix documentary series *Sex, Explained*, the "Birth Control" episode related a story of a doctor visiting a secluded

---

204 Not Educating Girls Costs Countries Trillions of Dollars," The World Bank.

205 "Gender Equality in Education, Employment and Entrepreneurship: Final Report to the MCM 2012," OECD, 2012.

Indonesian island village, and educating the women of the island about birth control and offering them such methods. A few years later, the society was richer and healthier due to the women having fewer complications surrounding birth and, therefore, living longer. Also, the ability to control the number of children they had meant they had more money to spend on the well-being of their existing families, including food, medicine, and other resources.[206]

A 2015 research study surrounding women in Ethiopia showed women's education had improved from 2005 to 2011. As one might guess, their education and work status were related to the quality of health for women, as well as their overall empowerment.[207] The authors of the study advise that those in positions of power, whether it be policymakers, planners, program managers, governmental/nongovernmental organizations, etc., should minimize the number of girls who either never attend school or drop out to marry.[208] Also, another survey on social development demonstrated that with this improvement in women's knowledge, it became more expected that they participate in national

---

206 "Birth Control," *Sex, Explained,* Netflix, Vox, January 2, 2020.

207 Masoumeh Simbar et al., "Comparison of Social, Economic and Familial Empowerment in Married Women in Three Cities of Iran," *International Journal of Community-Based Nursing and Midwifery* 5, no. 3 (2017): 248-255.

208 Yishak Abraham Lailulo, A. Sathiya Susuman, and Renette Blignaut, "Correlates of Gender Characteristics, Health and Empowerment of Women in Ethiopia," *BMC Women's Health* 15, no.116 (2015).

development projects.[209] It goes to show that not only does education improve the quality of life for women, but it also helps others recognize their potential to further contribute to society as well.

With so much research and evidence pointing to the benefits of educating young women, it begs the question: what can be done that hasn't already been done? Innovating new effective strategies will always be ideal, but for now, it can be beneficial to do what has been successful so far—advocating for the education of young women around the world.

Whether it be through campaigns, fundraisers, or non-profit organizations, it's important to keep it at the forefront of policymakers' minds. Creating policies that require non-discriminatory, free, and compulsory education for young women until they finish secondary school, at minimum, will provide the opportunity for young women to gain the skills and knowledge they need to create lives that are safe, fulfilling, and abundant. Not only do schools need to be built, but communities also need to be educated on why girls' education is so important. There are many negative stereotypes to unpack and refute respectfully for girls to safely continue their education.

Helping girls get into school isn't enough, either; helping them safely *stay* in school is another challenge to consider when implementing initiatives to educate young women. Funding scholarships and donating to offset costs of education will

---

209 Masoumeh Simbar et al., "Comparison of Social, Economic and Familial Empowerment..."

help girls get into school and, once in, continue their education without being pulled out or engaging in risky behavior, such as turning to sex work to pay their school fees.[210] Young girls are resorting to this behavior throughout the world, from Zimbabwe to the United Kingdom, and it's a lot more prevalent than one might initially think.[211] According to the National Student Money Survey in 2018, more than one in ten students "use their bodies" to make money when unexpectedly short of funds.[212]

While some do it by choice and safely, many are at risk for sexual violence, contracting diseases, and/or other negative consequences. No student should ever resort to using their bodies to pay for their education and related needs; it's a basic right that must be protected and provided for in safer ways. Creating policies and programs that make education more affordable is also a vital part of the effort; it's important to continually speak up for accessible, affordable, and quality education so it becomes a reality.

In the grand scheme of worldly issues, it may seem ridiculous to believe solutions can be found within a child's classroom.

---

210 Tarisai Chiyaka et al., "Reaching Young Women Who Sell Sex: Methods and Results of Social Mapping to Describe and Identify Young Women for DREAMS Impact Evaluation in Zimbabwe," PLOS ONE, March 15, 2018.

211 Eleanor Busby, "Students are Turning to Sex Work for Extra Money but Experts Warn Universities Are Ignoring the Issue," *Independent,* December 26, 2018.

212 Ruth Mushi, "Student Money Survey 2018 — Results," Save the Student, updated October 16, 2018.

But education is more than just learning abstract concepts and memorizing formulas and facts; it promotes self-confidence and self-sufficiency for a person.

Once again, P.H. Sethumadhava Rao illustrates the importance of education perfectly: "It brings light of hope; increases social, political, intellectual, cultural and religious consciousness; broadens the length of mind; removes all kinds of bigotry, narrowness, superstition and enhances fellow-feeling, tolerance, etc."[213] When we begin to work toward increasing access to education for young girls and women as a crucial aspect of their empowerment, we will witness these young women solving the problems that have been plaguing our global society for decades—and watch as they carry us to new heights.

213 P.H. Sethumadhava Rao, "Education for Women's Empowerment."

CHAPTER 11

IN THE WORKPLACE

Financially conscious. That's how my sisters and I would describe our upbringing. Our parents emphasized the value of managing money responsibly and encouraged us early in life to save—not spend—money that arrived in birthday cards and Christmas stockings. Now that I'm an adult, I value this life lesson. The fifteen-year-old version of myself, however, found the practice terribly inconvenient.

I was a social butterfly, not content to stay home and count the cash it was saving me. I wanted to get out of the house and hang out with friends. And maintaining a social life wasn't cheap, even at that age. I would need a job to bankroll my social calendar.

I continued to ration birthday and Christmas money for months, awaiting the day I could finally get my license. Then, that very morning, I forced my father to take me to the DMV, got my license, and went straight to work the first shift of my first job. Disregarding my parents' warnings about the struggle of customer service jobs, I had landed my own solution. That summer, I worked behind the counter at a sandwich shop.

I didn't initially take into account how exhausting it would be—the oddly scheduled hours, constantly being on my feet, and often working as one of the few people behind the counter during a lunch rush or closing shift. Yet even though I was exhausted after every shift and often drove home past midnight after closing the store, I felt deep satisfaction. With every payday, I was gaining more power over my own life!

With my own money, I could go out with my friends to eat, or buy clothes, or go to the movies without having to ask my parents to sponsor me. You see, before I got a job, they held a lot more power over my activities out of the house. After all, they insisted if it was their money, they had a say in how it would be spent, which I respected.

Since that summer, I've enjoyed the privilege of generally indulging in whatever I like without feeling guilty about spending someone else's money. It's one reason I've often held two jobs simultaneously and learned about money management to the point where my friends would ask me for advice. Money, to me, gave me the freedom to live the life I craved. A few years later, new circumstances eventually prevented me from holding a job, and I felt incredibly limited because I was reminded of how much our financial state affects our lives.

Many of us have heard the saying "money makes the world go 'round." As much as we might hate the idea, it's the reality of our society today. Without money, you can only do so much to improve your quality of life. Whether it be to access housing, healthy food, clothing, clean water, higher levels of education—almost everything requires money, whether you are the one paying or someone else is. Sadly, women are the most likely to be affected by a lack of income; among many poverty statistics, women and girls tend to be more affected than men, meaning more females tend to be in poverty-ridden situations than men.[214] According to the World Bank, 122 women between the ages of twenty-five and thirty-four live in poor households for every one hundred men of the same age group; it's just one of the many examples illustrating this disparity.[215]

Economic empowerment, therefore, is one of the most compelling strategies to empower women. It proves to be a powerful tool against poverty and levels the playing field when it comes to equitable access to resources. Also, acknowledging gender dynamics within the workplace often can be improved upon is critical. By leading efforts to create more economic opportunities for women throughout the globe and respecting their position in the workforce once they enter it, there is lot of room for economic prosperity and societal benefits.

ECONOMIC EMPOWERMENT
Women's economic empowerment refers to the process of achieving women's equal access to and control over economic

214 Carolina Sánchez- Páramo and Ana Maria Munoz-Boudet, "No, 70% of the World's Poor Aren't Women, but That Doesn't Mean Poverty Isn't Sexist," World Bank Blogs, March 8, 2018

215 Ibid.

resources,. It also includes having them use these resources to increase their exerted control over other areas of their lives.[216] Without being economically self-sufficient, other rights can become unattainable. This type of empowerment can free the poor, landless, deprived, and oppressed people throughout the world from all types of deprivation.[217] It allows them to directly enjoy the benefits of both markets and the household; they don't have to be limited to one or the other. They can afford the basic necessities, such as nutritious food, clothes, medicine, and clean water—and also other resources that will improve their standard of living, like professional development and training programs, loans to start small businesses, and more.

One organization strives to create a holistic sense of economic empowerment for poor women in India, believing that raising the visibility and voices of such women is not possible until universal access and ownership of economic resources exist for poor women. The Self-Employed Women's Association (SEWA) seeks to emphasize the economic empowerment of women. It aims to help female workers in India reach "full employment." This entails helping the workers obtain work and income security, food security, and social security (in minimal terms of health care, childcare, and shelter). It also desires to promote self-reliance among these women, in forms of being autonomous and having minimal

216 Georgia Taylor and Paola Pereznieto, "Review of Evaluation Approaches and Methods Used by Interventions on Women And Girls' Economic Empowerment," Overseas Development Institute, March 2014.

217 Keshab Chandra Mandal, "Concept and Types of Women Empowerment," *International Forum of Teaching and Studies* 9, no. 2 (2013).

dependence on others, both economically and in terms of their decision-making habits.[218]

Accumulating assets is also another avenue that fosters a sense of economic independence and can drastically change the quality of life for many women. Dr. Promilla Kapur, author of several books such as *Marriage and the Working Woman of India*, observes that "women's empowerment could be described as a process in which women gain a greater share of control over resources." She goes on to explain such resources vary; they can be material, human, and intellectual like knowledge, information, ideas, or financial resources like access to an income.[219] Economic independence does give women power and control over their own lives, which should be an innate right rather than a privilege.

The type of job can also impact the empowerment of women; it's not enough to simply hand them a low-income job in horrible working conditions and then wipe our hands clean. Women should be guaranteed safe and respectful working conditions, with fair hours, wages, and benefits, no matter where they are in the world or what position in society they may occupy. No woman should have to compromise on any one of these rights to make an income; we must stop exploiting women to increase the profits of a business or to continue to hold power over them.

---

218 "About Us," Self Employed Women's Association (SEWA), accessed June 9, 2020.

219 Keshab Chandral Mandal, "Concepts and Types of Women Empowerment."

We also should provide equal opportunity for women to perform the same jobs as men. According to UN Women, over 2.7 billion women are legally restricted from having the same job choices as men.[220] Many of these job choices provide the most income within their communities; if women can't have access to them, how are they supposed to take advantage of better financial opportunities? Often, people attempt to cite biological differences in men and women as a reason to allocate certain jobs to one sex over the other. "Women's jobs" tend to cite requirements (based on stereotypes) like less physical strength, more dexterity, less emotional stability, and involving less risk for potential offspring.[221] However, these conditions are just as harmful to men as they are to women. It allows employers to justify lower salaries and often boring tasks to women, while simultaneously rationalizing men's exposure to risky and dangerous working conditions.

Fortunately, many NGOs are creating efforts to bring women into previously male-dominated careers. CARE, a global humanitarian organization focused on defeating poverty and achieving social justice, has economic empowerment programs placed across the world to help women break the poverty cycle.[222] One such story happened in Lenche Wedyssa, Ethiopia, where a woman named Nuriya Yonis became a widow about twenty years ago. Left with six children to

---

220 "Facts and Figures: Economic Empowerment," UN Women, accessed June 9, 2020.

221 Karen Messing, "Do Men and Women Have Different Jobs Because of Their Biological Differences?" *International Journal of Health Services* 12, no.1 (1982).

222 "Mission and Vision," CARE, accessed June 9, 2020.

fend for, she found CARE, where she received—among other things—training on money-saving strategies and an opportunity to be an active participant in the local economy. Nuriya, in turn, provided a stable new life for her family. And it was all made possible with the help of honeybees.[223]

Not long ago, her success story would have been all but *impossible* to achieve in her Ethiopian community. Honey activities were male dominated in the area in which she lived, making it difficult for women to enter the space as workers. But through their beehive collective, CARE Ethiopia members supplied Nuriya and other women with bees, modern equipment, and training. Nuriya not only saved her money but also bought additional beehives to increase her earnings. Because of the economic assistance provided by CARE, she now can dream bigger and grow her business even more.[224]

CARE is also working to create attitudinal change to bring marginalized and landless women into the space. In many areas, the exclusion of women, especially marginalized groups like those left without property, creates a great challenge for them to access work. According to the United Nations, land is considered one of the most important economic assets, yet women only account for 12.8 percent of agricultural landholders across the world.[225] However, if

---

223 Nuriya Yonis, "Fighting Poverty & Drought with Honeybees," interviewed by CARE, uploaded November 11, 2011, YouTube Video.

224 Nuriya Yonis, "Fighting Poverty & Drought with Honeybees," interviewed by CARE, uploaded November 11, 2011, YouTube Video.

225 Ana Paula de la O Campos and Nynne Warring, "Gender and Land Statistics: Recent Developments in FAO's Gender and Land Rights Database,"

programs are created to account for this disparity and provide equal opportunity, we will be taking a great step toward providing financial stability and opportunity for growth for both women and their communities.

Protecting women's equal access to paid work provides a chance for women to level the playing field and become active participants in their economies. They can further spread important messages of advocacy if they hold high positions in national, state, or local institutions. This is because as they occupy higher-level jobs, their exposure to the media and other groups of people exponentially increases. Their impact upon their communities could be multiplied innumerably if simply given the chance to use their talents and intellect in the economic areas they've been historically denied access to.

Providing women the opportunity to be part of the larger workforce outside the domestic sphere is a challenge. And the obstacles don't end once women are allowed to take advantage of economic opportunities; they merely present themselves differently.

IN THE WORKFORCE

For many women, especially young women, it feels as though we are often corralled into taking certain jobs or pursuing certain careers. Much of this has to do with gender bias, such as the idea that "girls are not as good at hard sciences and mathematics as boys are," or that women cannot be effective leaders. Many more reasons include the lack of opportunity,

---

FAO, United Nations, 2015.

the need to find something—anything—that provides an income, and the amount of education necessary to occupy a specific position. Globally, women are more than capable of performing high-quality work in any sector. But even when presented the opportunity to take higher-level positions, women still question whether they should seize it.

The right way to pick a career doesn't exist. Each individual comes to the table with different backgrounds, endowments, struggles, values, and priorities. Let those inform your decision. Whether you choose your career for financial purposes, for the flexibility it provides, or for the fulfillment of your passions, pursue it without hesitation, as long as it's *your choice*. And should there come a time when your career and your purpose no longer align, don't panic. The choice to change jobs multiple times throughout a lifetime is yours to make too.

We constantly hear about the lack of women in STEM (Science, Technology, Engineering, and Mathematics) fields. According to the UNESCO Institution for Statistics, less than 30 percent of the world's researchers are women.[226] While the number of women graduating with STEM degrees is increasing, they still constitute only around a quarter of the STEM workforce globally.[227] Black women, Latina women, and other racially underrepresented groups comprise only

---

226 "Women in Science," UNESCO Institute for Statistics, UNESCO, accessed June 9, 2020.

227 Sarah Feldman, "Steady Rise for Women in STEM but Gender Gap Remains," Statista, February 11, 2019, "The State of Girls and Women in STEM," National Girls Collaborative Project, March 2018.

5 percent of those working in STEM fields today. These statistics don't reflect the actual aptitude of young women in STEM.[228] In a study involving data from sixty-seven countries, girls scored as well as, if not better than, boys on science exams and would have been capable of college-level science and math classes, had they enrolled.[229]

Young women should be able to pursue careers that align with their interests and strengths. Even once you have secured a position in the workforce, you'll find this passion will serve as your rock to withstand the coming struggles. So don't be intimidated by a male-dominated field. Pursue your purpose.

Even when women have rightfully secured their position in a career of their choosing, they often encounter skeptics, intent on diminishing their capability, contributions, and value. Harassment, lack of acknowledgment, or other social dynamics that work against a woman's success can seem like a never-ending battle. No matter how male-dominated a field may be, it must provide a culture in which women, too, feel their knowledge, bodies, ideas, thoughts, and feelings are respected. Microaggressions shouldn't be normalized, and harassment should never be tolerated. If these are present in the workplace, perpetrators need to be held accountable. And accountability requires a collective effort from all members of an organization, at all levels.

---

228 Ibid.

229 Gijsbert Stoet and David C. Geary, "The Gender-Equality Paradox in Science, Technology, Engineering, and Mathematics Education," *Psychological Science* 29, no. 4 (2018).

One female leader who spoke to me about her journey noted the value of the open and informative environment that exists within her male-dominated workplace. Jumirna Ramirez, an activist passionate about addressing the effects of gentrification, found her voice within Uptown Progressive Action (UPA). She said she really learned the fundamentals of community organizing there. "UPA opened the door to opportunities and learning about different bigger issues. It gave me a platform to express my concerns and learn where these problems [with gentrification] are coming from," she said. For Jumirna, this organization finally let her explore the issues that mattered to her, from housing to health care to education. "If it weren't for them," she declared, "I would be struggling to express my concerns and be vocal when I need help."

Rather than provide a hostile work environment, UPA provided the space and support for Jumirna to flourish as an organizer and activist in her community. "I knew there was something wrong, but I didn't know the background of the issue, what to do, what resources existed, or the networks that they had." With UPA consistently reminding Jumirna of the power of her voice, she found a passion for policymaking and seeks to create an effective policy that leads to social impact. Her role within UPA started as an internship and has evolved into a mentorship, with opportunities to conduct webinars that focus on the quality of health care, health disparities, health injustices, and other health issues.

Jumirna realized that even if she receives opposition when entering the political space, her work environment gave her the clarity and resolve to persist regardless of the challenges she will face. "I think I can take the heat because that's what society wants. They want minority/colored women to be afraid of speaking up, or they'll try to intimidate them and put them in a corner. It's because we have real narratives, and people don't want us to tell the stories that relate to the issues that exist." Jumirna recognizes people will constantly seek to silence and/or invalidate her. However, she refuses to cower in the face of that challenge and encourages young women to speak up for themselves and actively counter these discrediting efforts.

It can't just be women calling out such behavior; men need to keep each other accountable as well. Silence will only help the perpetrator, and it isn't just a "woman's issue." The entire organization benefits when men become involved in gender equity practices. Research shows that when men are deliberately engaged in gender inclusion programs, 96 percent of organizations see progress—compared to only 30 percent of organizations where men are not engaged.[230] Gender inclusion comes in many forms; it means refraining from making sexist jokes, allowing women to speak uninterrupted at meetings, giving due credit to female colleagues for ideas/presentations/proposals/etc. It's about ensuring women feel like valued and respected members of an organization, without having to compromise their identity as women to do so.

---

230 Matt Krentz et al., "Five Ways Men Can Improve Gender Diversity at Work," Boston Consulting Group, October 10, 2017.

COLLEGE CAMPUSES COUNT TOO

While academic settings are different from work environments for multiple reasons, similar issues arise and must be accounted for and addressed. Whether it's the rise of reported sexual assaults on campuses or that women in STEM courses don't feel as valued or as welcomed, a young woman attending college is forced to become aware of all the potential struggles and hurdles they may face.

While women in college are perceived as more empowered, and they are in the sense that they have an opportunity to achieve a higher level of education, they are still vulnerable to attacks on their person. The statistic that one in five women will be sexually assaulted while in college is terrifying. While these numbers may vary based on location, university, and survey respondents, this doesn't negate the fact that the prevalence of such an issue is universal.[231] And not only that, around 80 percent of sexual assault victims *don't* report the assault in college.[232]

Studies have shown this comes from the victim's variety of doubts; many don't have confidence in the college administration to handle it properly, which may be related to the fact that most colleges either fail to report or under-report

---

231   Michele C. Black et al., *The National Intimate Partner and Sexual Violence Survey (NISVS): 2010 Summary Report,* National Center for Injury Prevention and Control, Centers for Disease Control and Prevention, November 2011.

232   "Campus Sexual Violence: Statistics," RAINN, accessed June 9, 2020.

such crimes.[233] Many victims also aren't even aware their experience constitutes sexual assault or rape, or they may fear people will not support or believe them. In other cases, they may fear they'll be blamed by authorities or put on trial and, consequently, subject to public scrutiny.

Before I started college, I would hear about the "one in five" statistic all the time. Yet I had always believed it would never happen to someone I knew because it was the only way I could walk around without being in constant fear for myself or my loved ones. But this ignorance couldn't last forever because, within a few weeks of starting college, I started getting phone calls in the middle of the night.

Even if it had been months since we had talked, I wouldn't even get out a "Hello?" before hearing sobbing on the other end of the line. I'd sit there, miles away from the friends I loved, unable to offer them anything but the sound of my voice and tears as I cried with them. They told me of how terrified they were because they didn't know what next steps to take or feared being put in the public eye. They told me about how their academic institutions didn't have effective policies regarding this issue or that they'd witnessed how perpetrators often only received a slap on the wrist for such aggression.

I wish it had only been one phone call, but I've received several over the past few years, and I can't even count the

233 Nell Gluckman, "Students Say They Don't Trust Campus Title IX Pro-
     cesses. And They Doubt Their Own Reports Would Be Taken Seriously,"
     The Chronicle of Higher Education, October 23, 2019, "An Underreported
     Problem: Campus Sexual Misconduct," AAUW, accessed June 9, 2020.

number of crying young women I've held in my arms as they endure the long-lasting effects of such a painful experience. No matter how much I listen, how much consolation I try to offer, it will never be enough to fully heal what they've gone through. I don't want to receive these calls and only be able to offer empathy. I want my friends and fellow young women to enter these environments without fearing for their personal safety, without having to fight for their respect. This is why I believe we, as a society, need to become more insistent that change is *implemented,* not just promised.

Colleges, and especially the men in these settings, need to condemn these aggressions. Efforts need to be made toward creating a safer environment for women to *live their lives,* let alone pursue their education. Remember, respect and safety for women shouldn't be considered privileges; they should be deemed human rights. This can come in the form of promoting gender-inclusion programs and initiatives, and teaching students about their rights as a student and person from the moment they step onto campus or, even better, before they reach college. As I mentioned in previous chapters, it's about shifting the mentality of how we should view women and their rights. Addressing the roots of these negative mindsets will lead to lasting behavioral changes and, therefore, cultural changes in our society.

Institutions should prioritize raising student and faculty awareness on what a culture of gender equality looks like. But raising awareness must be coupled with demonstrated efforts to minimize the present inequalities. Encouraging incidence reporting, no matter the level of aggression, is yet another way to move toward gender equality. These reports should be followed up with published records of such incidences rather than allowing them to perpetuate in silence. We need to hold people accountable for their actions and the lasting effects of the crimes they commit.

For women, any place can be a battleground—their homes, their communities, their workplaces, their classrooms. We must make efforts to give women the chance to fight for what they deserve. Economically empowering women and creating more respectful and safe work/academic environments would do wonders to relieve the current plight of women throughout the world. It's imperative they not only are given quality opportunities but also are free to pursue them without being concerned about whether they will be respected as human beings. However, we are not helpless—by banding together and making a collective effort, we can use our resources to implement changes that will provide women, and therefore our society as a whole, a chance to prosper.

CHAPTER 12

SPEAK UP & SHOW UP

———

As Imxn waited for the screen to load, she could swear her heartbeat picked up a little. This was her first virtual meeting with Global Girlhood, an up-and-coming civic and social organization, and Imxn was debuting as the group's new Public Relations Coordinator. In her new role, she'd use storytelling and social media to connect and engage womxn of all ages and identities.[234] And while she was excited about her new adventure, she couldn't help but feel a little anxious as well. What would the environment be like? Would she *finally* have coworkers with whom she could relate? And if all the work would be done remotely, how could they even build community?

Moments later, Imxn entered the online meeting room and, right away, she felt at home. She had been anxious, in part, because of past experiences that had proven disappointing.

---

234 "Womxn" – meaning women or woman (depending on context); used as an alternative spelling to avoid the suggestion of sexism perceived in the sequences *m-a-n* and *m-e-n*, and to be inclusive of trans and nonbinary women. "Womxn," Dictionary.com, accessed June 10, 2020.

In those gatherings with other girls, she'd felt a competitive ambiance and a reluctance to share her ideas and opinions. This, she could already sense, would be different. Global Girlhood felt welcoming. She didn't know all the girls in the online room yet, but she could feel the power of this community of women, clearly committed to the organization's mission. The girls listened respectfully and shared their ideas enthusiastically. As the meeting progressed, Imxn felt inspired, safe, comfortable, and—for the first time in a long time—connected. She had at last found the people she had always hoped to work with!

I asked Imxn to recommend one powerful way to make an impact that will lift up women. Her advice? Create community. Being able to thrive and work in a safe, open-minded, and respectful environment with her peers allowed her to explore her passions and express herself, and it strengthened her network. But she also recognized there was space to improve the community as well.

"Even with Global Girlhood being diverse, I was the only Latina there. I feel responsible to get my community involved, which includes performing outreach to the Latina community," she explained. Since Global Girlhood is a virtual platform, I asked how she could perform that outreach and feel a connection with the target audience. While social media can make us more connected in a certain sense, I had found it difficult to feel I was communicating well through it.

"Well, for a start," Imxn began, "I'll try talking about the issues that relate to women of color and me, and then invite them to talk and be engaged on my social media posts. Often, people are very hesitant because they feel like they don't belong in that conversation, or that they're not 'qualified' enough." But while she sometimes struggles with getting a strong response from her target demographic, she's learned to look for the small wins. "I'm successful when just one person shows that they were positively impacted," she declared, "like if they felt invited or that they mattered."

I once believed I was incapable of making an impact. I thought if I couldn't be at the forefront of a movement or in the middle of a relief effort, my contributions wouldn't effect change. Pranjal, Imxn, and Elyse have demonstrated change doesn't only emanate from the thick of a resource-scarce area. We can fight for female empowerment and create social change from anywhere in the world.

Start by finding communities built around social issues that resonate with you, like Imxn found in Global Girlhood. Joining like-minded individuals in a shared interest may connect you to opportunities to help make the change you seek. You can also positively impact others through volunteering or interning at an organization. Whether you give your time and energy to efforts for girls' education, improved access to clean water, economic empowerment of rural female business owners, or another issue that resonates with you, volunteers fuel the engine to keep many of these initiatives running.

Any type of support can snowball into a larger impact. Participate in demonstrations and marches, as the more people involved, the more attention the issue gets.

If the community you're searching for doesn't already exist, create one. Organize events in support of the cause that's important to you, and similar-minded supporters will find *you*. That's precisely what Deja Foxx did when she created the GenZ Girl Gang. She began by defining her objectives: to connect young, female-identifying people who wanted to (1) support other womxn and (2) create change through education and collaboration. Today, the Gang boasts over nine thousand followers and provides resources on a variety of different social issues.

You can also use your voice to make an impact. Amplify the message or issue through social media and word of mouth. Most people are rationally ignorant—it's impossible for EVERYONE to stay abreast of EVERY injustice in the world, let alone know what they can do about it. Fortunately, you can bring that injustice to the forefront of their minds with consistent tweets, updates, or reposts. While the action itself is simple and takes only a few seconds, millions of people across the world have been reached this way, and it shows technology can be used to our advantage if we use it effectively.

Wherever you are, pressure your policymakers to take action and address the problems that plague our society. Call, text, mail letters, sign petitions, or even show up to their door and lobby them in person. You can also support campaigns and initiatives through financial contributions, as most non-profit organizations and other advocacy organizations rely on donations and sponsorship to continue their work and expand their impact. Considering the thousands of organizations that exist, at least one likely resonates with you, and your contribution doesn't have to be enormous to still lead toward a better future.

We don't discuss political empowerment enough, even though it may be the most effective way to empower women.[235] Political representation and activity put these issues on the agendas of policymakers. Not only this—for women to be truly empowered, they must participate at all levels of government. Women face countless struggles daily; whether through encountering subjugation, oppression, or ill treatment both within and outside their familial unit, the obstacles for women have no end. Many women around the world dream of the privileged lives many of us are fortunate to have. If women can't sit at the political "table" where they can formulate programs and policies that relate to their challenges, they will continue to struggle to survive.

Politics influences the distribution of resources. If we involve more women politically, we can decentralize power and authority. This, in turn, helps the deprived and oppressed people who couldn't participate in the decision-making processes beforehand. They can then help determine program implementation strategies ranging from government policy to familial and social issues.

To learn more about how imperative political empowerment is for women, Dr. Deondra Rose and I explored how integral politics are to advancing the position of women in society, especially within democracies like the United States. "In a

---

235 Keshab Chandra Mandal, "Concept and Types of Women Empowerment," *International Forum of Teaching and Studies* 9, no. 2 (2013).

democratic form of government," she said, "one of the central pillars of the entire endeavor is that power ultimately rests with the people." The actions the government takes are intended to be "what the people wish to see done."

Unfortunately, "the people" often don't get an equal say on how the government uses the country's resources. In a nation where about 51 percent of the population is composed of women, America's halls of powers show women are sorely underrepresented.[236] Whether in corporate or political leadership, even though women are full participants in the day-to-day operations in societies, families, households, and communities, our presence doesn't necessarily translate into equitable access to political power. Women have been steadily increasing their presence in Congress in recent years (close to 24 percent as of 2020), yet we've never had a female vice president or president.237

"When you really parse it through," Dr. Rose relayed to me, "there's a large and long history of gender inequality in politics and government. That has important outcomes for how we treat women, how our institutions reflect the needs of women, and the inclusion of women's voices."

So what can we do to politically empower women? Dr. Rose offered suggestions based on her experience and knowledge:

236 U.S. Census Bureau, "Quick Facts: United States – Age and Sex," accessed June 10, 2020.

237 "Women in the U.S. Congress 2020," Rutgers Eagleton Institute of Politics, accessed June 10, 2020.

- Never stop learning – "Learn from the interviews, from the lived experiences of people who are like you and nothing like you, in community, background, priorities, etc. We have to work so much harder in this historical moment to connect with people and people who are different from us. But if we make the consistent choice to expose ourselves to people whom we can learn from, the more we can connect with people and learn in meaningful ways about their experiences to understand where they're coming from. The better we can listen and connect, the more good we can do as problem solvers."

- Don't hold back – "If you see a problem, fix it! We wait for a perfect moment, thinking, 'I'm not qualified enough,' or 'I don't have anything to say.' But it's especially those who are interested in topic and research that are needed, because the people who are in the debate often don't bring in any knowledge or lived experience the way many of us can."

- Mass engagement in politics – "Those who engage in politics on the mass level are more likely to see outcomes in the political process reflect their interest. For example, senior citizens often are really involved, and, therefore, the government tends to prioritize their interests." If we all start to prioritize political involvement, we will make strides in creating policy change that allows for marginalized groups, especially women, to exercise full and equal participation as citizens.

Even the simple act of voting can create a tsunami of change. Vote for candidates who support women's rights. Vote women into political positions. Vote for the rights of women and girls, and make sure they're on policymakers' agendas. A simple ballot can set the precedent for years of potential changes being implemented.

Unfortunately, many factors continue to hinder women's political participation. For example, women may lack the time to vote, depending on their domestic and/or professional workload. They may lack confidence, education, and/or consciousness. They may doubt the importance of their own vote or question whether they are suitable to take up political positions. In some countries, women may lack the financial positions required to vote within their communities. Even an age-old belief, custom, or superstition can deter women from voting. Across the world, women continue to be subject to hostile societies that don't wish for them to have a say.

If you believe our society fully participates in political elections, the Pew Research Center has news for you. It reported that only 56 percent of the U.S. voting-age population cast ballots in the 2016 presidential election, making it one of the lowest rates among developed countries.[238] That means only about half of the country's eligible voters actually cast a vote, and that's only within the United States in recent years.

In a study conducted by the UN spanning 103 countries/areas, women's representation in elected local deliberative bodies varied from less than 1 percent to close to parity (50 percent), with a median of 26 percent.[239] We must encourage women

---

238 Drew DeSilver, "U.S. Trails Most Developed Countries in Voter Turnout," *Fact Tank,* Pew Research Center, May 21, 2018.

239 United Nations, "The Sustainable Development Goals Report 2019," United Nations, 2019.

to vote, and if they can't, those who can vote should strive to advocate for women and the issues that disproportionately affect them.

Above all else, do not stay silent. In this world, you only get what you ask for, or better yet, what you demand. While people in power may acknowledge the need to elevate the status of women, they often put it on the back burner until we pressure them to take action. Moving toward gender equality and creating a more equitable world for women requires involvement from supporters at all levels. For a cause as important as this one, there is no such thing as being too far removed from it. Our world has allowed us the opportunity to connect more than ever before. We have the tools and resources to aid a movement no matter where we live, and we must take hold of this potential and use it for the greater good.

FINAL WORDS

———

Before anything else, I want to first say thank you.

Thank you for taking the time to pick up this book, to peruse its pages, and to ponder upon not only why female empowerment is important but what you can do to support the women in your life. While it may not seem like it, just opening this book was the first step to becoming a better ally, leader, and changemaker.

As I continue learning more and more about the various challenges societies face across the world, I become more firm in my belief that female empowerment can solve many of our problems. We live in a reality where more than three billion people live on less than $2.50 a day, and more than a third live on even less.[240] Women and girls are some of the most vulnerable people in poverty, as they lack the resources and rights to break the cycle.

———

240 United Nations Development Programme, "Sustaining Human Progress: Reducing Vulnerabilities and Building Resilience," Human Development Report, 2014.

We've known for years that female empowerment is necessary. The Jakarta Declaration, which was created at the Fourth International Conference on Health Promotion (attended by World Health Organization Member States), examined that the empowerment of women should not only consist of equal consideration—it is a necessary precondition for sustainable economic and social development, which, in turn, leads to health promotion.[241]

It's been over two decades since this global plan was made, and it continues to be relevant to our society today. As Melinda Gates stated in her book, *The Moment of Lift*, "If you want to lift up humanity, empower women. It is the most comprehensive, pervasive, high-leverage investment you can make in human beings."[242]

Throughout this book, you've seen how social change has evolved over the years and has been one of the only constants through time and across societies. Our world refuses to be the same for even a moment; no matter where we are, a change is being made, for better or for worse. The important thing is to encourage the involvement of people to make the positives outweigh the negatives.

Millions of young women hold the key to lifting our communities up; we can't let them stay in the shadows any longer. They are strong, intelligent, capable, and determined, but

---

241 "Jakarta Declaration on Leading Health Promotion into the 21st Century," World Health Organization, accessed June 10, 2020.

242 Melinda Gates, *The Moment of Lift: How Empowering Women Changes the World*, (New York: Flatiron Books, 2019). p.27.

many barriers stand in their way. But, as you've read, female empowerment isn't about just handing women resources and opportunities with minimal thought and effort.

This book is just the first step to creating change. It touched on dozens of global challenges, yet there are hundreds more to be addressed. My hope is that you will go forward and choose to learn more about social impact and the ways we can come together to shift our society to becoming more equal. Take the time to learn about the various problems you've been exposed to and actively look for ways to become part of the movement to ameliorate those issues.

Women deserve to be healthy and have enough to meet their own needs, as well as the needs of those they care about. Every woman should be able to live with respect and dignity. They should be able to live and work in safe environments that encourage their overall growth and development. We need to understand supporting women requires efforts for equality in *all* sectors of life. We can't just pick and choose what is considered female empowerment depending on what is most convenient.

But that doesn't mean all hope is lost. In fact, I hope you've realized we are living in a time of great opportunity. If we can mobilize and come together to support women, and especially young women, we have a chance to create strides in any sector we can think of—political, economic, health, you name it, empowering women will only make it better. Once we start allowing women across the globe to contribute just as much as men have been allowed, we move toward eliminating the domination, oppression, and discrimination the female population has suffered for centuries.

As spiritual leader and social reformer Swami Vivekananda once said so eloquently, "Countries and nations which do not respect women have never become great nor will ever be in the future."[243] We have come very far as a global society, but we still have far to go. But now that you have the knowledge and tools to help implement positive change, I hope you take it and start looking for ways to make an impact in your own community. Remember, there's value in changing one life, even if it's simply your own.

And for my fellow young women, I have a special message for you:

You have been a great part of the past, and you are our future. The world has gone on too long without universally recognizing the equality of the genders, and change is overdue. Every single one of you can make an impact, and it starts with recognizing your own strength and power. None of us escape this world without facing challenges; it's one of the universal burdens of being a human, and it's amplified when you are a woman because many people don't want you to succeed. But for every person who wishes for you to fail, dozens more are hoping you not only overcome these obstacles but thrive within them. You can achieve whatever you set your mind to; it will never be easy, but it will always be worth it.

---

243 Purvaja Mahadevan, "Empowering Women Rebuilding the Society," Civil Service India, accessed June 10, 2020.

Stand up and pursue the things you dream of and the things you deserve. Refuse to believe the world is against you; see other women as your friends, as your biggest supporters, as people who can connect with you on a level no man ever can. And besides those women, understand other people also want to be your allies and will do everything in their power to help you receive the rights you deserve. You don't always have to see eye to eye, but you should always be respectful of each other. Work toward a world where every girl's voice is heard, where it never crosses her mind to ever wish she wasn't a woman.

Women have endured endless suffering with unimaginable resilience, but we can implement changes that diminish this suffering as much as we can. A world is waiting for us where we are seen as equals, where we command respect regardless of our economic status, where our experiences are never invalidated. It's possible, I promise. All you have to do is one simple thing.

Rise.

ACKNOWLEDGMENTS

———

First and foremost, I have to give thanks to God. While I may not have always known what I was doing during this journey, He did, and for that, I'm eternally grateful.

Next, I want to thank my family, who tried their best to tiptoe around me as we were all self-quarantined at home together. Amma, thank you for being my work buddy and for bringing me chaya and forcing me to eat when I got too focused. Dad, thanks for always relieving my stress by casually saying the craziest things. You continue to provide silly memories that I can still laugh (and write!) about years later. Seona and Sharon Chech, thank you for your unwavering support throughout this whole process. You even tried to help me with my citations! Even though neither of you read my instructions and ended up doing them wrong, at least we got a good cry-laughing session out of it. I'm happy to be home with all of you.

Thank you to all my interviewees, who took time out of their busy schedules to share their stories with me. Your passion, intellect, and dedication to creating social impact have inspired me more than you know. And yes, that means I'll continue to gush about all of you until the day I die.

Thank you to my close friends who constantly reminded me to stop being intimidated by my dreams. I will be eternally grateful for all the late-night pep talks you gave me. Your constant encouragement and excitement for *Rise* would serve to remind me why I wanted to write this book in the first place. I hope it's as wonderful as you had hoped.

Thank you to New Degree Press, especially the incredibly energetic Eric Koester, the enthusiastic Brian Bries, my DE and unofficial personal therapist Cass Lauer, and editor/cheerleader extraordinaire Pea Richelle White! Thank you for your patience and for always showing up for me. This book would not have been possible without all of you.

Thank you to all the young women across the world who give me hope and are the inspiration behind this book. You will change the world, and I can't wait to witness it.

And finally, thank you to all the people who believed in me and came along on this journey. You have my immense gratitude for your generosity, encouragement, and support of my book. Thank you for believing not only in me but in the power of women everywhere. Let's change our world, together:

Simon Abraham	Phylicia Abraham
Sibia Abraham	Joseph (Thampy) Abraham
Seona Abraham	Ben Abraham
Sharon Abraham	Geethi Abraham

Mebin Abraham
Majesh and Lincy Abraham
Manoj Abraham
Ameen Ahmad
Ayesha Ahmad
Jennifer Alarcon
Aimee Allison
Jomoll Asok
Musa Ayyad
Izzy Bank
Julia Blankenbaker
Nico Bodkin
Ozi Boms
Michael Bundalo
Arianna Carr
Christopher Chacko
Seenu Chacko
Jenni Chackochen
Gurbhej Cheema
Cathy Chen
Benjamin Chilampath
Josie Cloud
Jeffna Elavumkal
Sherin Ellickal
Pilar Pulgar Ezquerra
Liza Francis
Beth Frost
Yvette Fuentes
Madhu Ganesh
Margaret Gawrych
Neetthu George
Sandya George

Lincy George
Riya Gilja
Megan Greenfield
Gabriela Gross
Angelo Guo
Jessica Huang
Robin Hulshizer
Simon Illikattil
Rachel Irengo
Betsy Jacob
Ceona James
Reethika James
Reen James
Jiji John
Jojoe and Cini John
Christeena Jojo
Priya Jose
Jincy Asha Jose
Jensy Joseph
Jenny Joseph
Brittney Joseph
Jasmine Joseph
Ashley Joseph
Gibu Joseph
Jensy Kalavelil
Danny Kaniyaly
Rani James Kattapuram
Reema Kavalackal
Aarthi Kaviyarasu
Sara Keith
Ashley Kim
Cheryl King

Eric Koester
Jeslyn Koovakada
Jacob Korah
Thresiamma Kunnacherril
Reshma Kurian
Bincy Kurian
Caitlin Lang
Pia Laudadio
Lizbeth Leapo
Brian Yinan Li
Linus Li
Terri Lindenberg
Catherine Livingston
Kim Bella Lobraco
Sarah LoCurto
Sheryl Lukose
Aliya Lukose
Ryesa Mansoor
Neelima Mathai
John Mathew
Sanil Mathew
Laura McGovern
Sydney Moore
Estella Muro
Kristi Njaravelil
Cinthia Ogbaugo
Julie Olzen
Morgan Olzen
Rajani Pallikunnel
Vimal Panalickal
Nicole Park
Jhanvi V. Patel

Leon Peter
Alice Philip
Matthew Philip
Jeremy Poothakary
Rachel Poothakary
Trisha Poothakary
Shobin Puthusseril
Alex Ragh
Lesley Rajan
Malavi Ravindran
Indira Reddy
Michaela Reinhart
Dominic Rose
Deondra Rose
Sera Sajan
Gaby Salvatore
Casey Samagalsky
Aaron Sandberg
Taylor Severino
Amanda Siciak
Julia Simon
Tesa Annu Taju
Eritrea Temesghen
Cynthia Thachettu
Leena Thalackal
Vinitha Thomas
Divya Thomas
Joban Thomas
Tony V Thomas
Tomy Thomas
Divya Vallippadavil
Shinu Varghese

Lucy Vayalil
Jaimie Vayalil
Lisa Vazhayil
Alexus Wells
Jacob White

Jamie Wiszniewski
Emilia Wojcikowski
Lauren Wozniak
Michael Xie
Christine Yang

APPENDIX

___

INTRODUCTION

Emerson, Sarah. "Empowered Women Are Key to Transforming Communities." *Project Concern International*, March 9, 2016. https://www.pciglobal.org/empowered-women-key-transforming-communities-2/.

FAO. *World Food and Agriculture Statistical Pocketbook 2018*. United Nations. https://www.globalagriculture.org/fileadmin/files/weltagrarbericht/Weltagrarbericht/10B%C3%A4uerlicheIndustrielleLW/Pocketbook2018.pdf.

Pramuk, Jacob. "Bill Clinton: Hillary Is 'The Best Darn Change-Maker I've Ever Known,'" *CNBC*. Updated July 27, 2016. https://www.cnbc.com/2016/07/26/bill-clinton-hillary-is-the-best-darn-change-maker-ive-ever-seen.html.

Hendricks, Benjamin. 2020. "What Is a Changemaker?" *Observations of a Changemaker*. Accessed June 8. https://changemakerobs.wordpress.com/what-is-a-changemaker/.

Reem Rahman, Kris Herbst, and Tim Scheu, "What Is a Change-maker?" *Fast Company*, August 4, 2016. https://www.fastcompany.com/3062483/what-is-a-changemaker.

UNFPA. "Adolescent and Youth Demographics: A Brief Overview." United Nations Population Fund. Accessed June 8, 2020. https://www.unfpa.org/sites/default/files/resource-pdf/One%20pager%20on%20youth%20demographics%20GF.pdf.

United Nations Sustainable Development Goals. "Goal 5: Achieve Gender Equality and Empower All Women and Girls." United Nations. Accessed June 8, 2020. https://www.un.org/sustainabledevelopment/gender-equality/.

CHAPTER 1

Amnesty International. "Yemen: Women's Rights Must Be Front and Center." Accessed June 8, 2020. https://www.amnestyusa.org/yemen-womens-rights-must-be-front-and-center/.

Carnevale, Anthony P., Nicole Smith, and Kathryn Peltier Campbell, "May the Best Woman Win? Education and Biases Against Women in American Politics," Georgetown University Center on Education and the Workforce, 2019. https://cew.georgetown.edu/wp-content/uploads/Women_in_Politics.pdf.

Center for Reproductive Rights. "The World's Abortion Laws." Accessed June 8, 2020. https://reproductiverights.org/worldabortionlaws?country=NIC&category[294]=294.

Clark, Nancy F. "Act Now to Shrink the Confidence Gap." *Forbes.* April 28, 2014. https://www.forbes.com/sites/womens-media/2014/04/28/act-now-to-shrink-the-confidence-gap/#-5daeb1425c41.

Clinton Global Initiative. "Empowering Girls and Women" "Empowering Girls and Women," United Nations Economic and Social Council. Accessed June 8, 2020. https://www.un.org/en/ecosoc/phlntrpy/notes/clinton.pdf.

Gebhardt, Jillesa. "On Equal Pay Day 2019, Lack of Awareness Persists." *Curiosity at Work (blog)*. Survey Monkey. Accessed June 8, 2020. https://www.surveymonkey.com/curiosity/equal-pay-day-2019/.

Kay, Katty and Claire Shipman. "The Confidence Gap." *The Atlantic*, May 2014. https://www.theatlantic.com/magazine/archive/2014/05/the-confidence-gap/359815/.

Lindeman, Meghan I. H., Amanda M. Durik, and Maura Dooley. "Women and Self-Promotion: A Test of Three Theories." *Psychological Reports* 122, no. 1 (2019): 219-230. https://doi.org/10.1177%2F0033294118755096.

Merriam-Webster, s.v. "Impostor Syndrome (*n*.)." Accessed June 8, 2020. https://www.merriam-webster.com/dictionary/impostor%20syndrome.

Mlambo-Ngcuka, Phumzile. "Women Are Change-Makers." UN Women. October 20, 2016. https://www.unwomen.org/en/news/stories/2016/10/speech-by-executive-director-at-opening-ceremony-of-iifmena-conference.

Murdock, Jason. "'Hillary's Gone Crazy'": Trump Defends Tulsi Gabbard after Clinton Says Democratic Candidate Is Being 'Groomed' by Russia." *Newsweek,* October 10, 2019. https://www.newsweek.com/donald-trump-defends-tulsi-gabbard-hillary-clinton-groomed-russia-1466503.

"Overconfident Men," *Utah Women and Leadership Project (blog),* Utah Valley University, August 27, 2015. https://www.uvu.edu/uwlp/blog/overconfident-men.html.

Page, Nanette and Cheryl E. Czuba. "Empowerment: What Is It?" *Journal of Extension* 37, no. 5 (1999). https://joe.org/joe/1999october/comm1.php.

Povoledo, Elisabetta. "Vatican Faces Modern-Day Suffragists, Demanding Right to Vote." *The New York Times,* October 26, 2018. https://www.nytimes.com/2018/10/26/world/europe/vatican-women-leadership.html?auth=login-email&login=email.

Rudman, Laurie A. and Julie E. Phelan. "Backlash Effects for Disconfirming Gender Stereotypes in Organizations." Research in Organizational Behavior 28, (2008): 61-79. https://doi.org/10.1016/j.riob.2008.04.003.

Sandberg, Sheryl. *Lean In: Women, Work, and the Will to Lead.* New York, New York: Random House Audio, 2013.

The Water Project. "The Water Crisis: Education in Africa." Accessed June 8, 2020. https://thewaterproject.org/why-water/education.

World Health Organization. "Gender." Accessed June 8, 2020. https://www.who.int/health-topics/gender.

CHAPTER 2

Blakemore, Erin. "What Was the Arab Spring and How Did It Spread?" *National Geographic*. March 19, 2019. https://www.nationalgeographic.com/culture/topics/reference/arab-spring-cause/.

Blakemore, Erin. "Youth in Revolt: Five Powerful Movements Fueled by Young Activists." *National Geographic*. March 23, 2018. https://www.nationalgeographic.com/news/2018/03/youth-activism-young-protesters-historic-movements/.

Cain, Rachel. "Five Reasons to Be Cheerful about Young People and Social Change." *Sheila McKechnie Foundation*, March 19, 2019. https://smk.org.uk/five-reasons-cheerful-young-people-social-change/.

Chuck, Elizabeth, Alex Johnson, and Corky Siemaszko. "17 Killed in Mass Shooting at High School in Parkland, Florida." *NBC News*. February 14, 2019. https://www.nbcnews.com/news/us-news/police-respond-shooting-parkland-f=lorida-high-school-n848101.

Cobb, Charlie. "Challenging White Power." *SNCC Digital Gateway*. Accessed June 8, 2020. https://snccdigital.org/inside-sncc/the-story-of-sncc/challenging-white-power/.

Encyclopaedia Britannica Online. Academic ed., s.v. "Arab Spring." Accessed on June 10, 2020. https://www.britannica.com/event/Arab-Spring.

Encyclopaedia Britannica Online. Academic ed., s.v. "Mohamed Bouazizi." Accessed on June 10, 2020. https://www.britannica.com/biography/Mohamed-Bouazizi.

Encyclopaedia Britannica Online. Academic ed., s.v. "Montgomery Bus Boycott to the Voting Rights Act," by Carson, Clayborne. Accessed on June 8, 2020. https://www.britannica.com/event/American-civil-rights-movement/From-black-power-to-the-assassination-of-Martin-Luther-King.

Encyclopaedia Britannica Online, Academic ed., s.v. "Social Change," by Form, William and Wilterdink, Nick. Accessed June 8, 2020. https://www.britannica.com/topic/social-change.

"Gates Foundation Poll Finds Young People More Optimistic About Future Than Older Generations; Optimism Highest in Lower- and Middle-Income Countries," *Bill and Melinda Gates Foundation.* September 24, 2018. https://www.gatesfoundation.org/Media-Center/Press-Releases/2018/09/Gates-Foundation-Poll-Finds-Young-People-More-Optimistic-About-Future-Than-Older-Generation.

Griffith, James. "Tiananmen Square: World Marks 30 Years Since Tiananmen Massacre as China Censors All Mention." *CNN.* June 4, 2019. https://www.cnn.com/2019/06/03/asia/tiananmen-june-4-china-censorship-intl/index.html.

Jones, Maggie. "The March for Our Lives Activists Showed Us How to Find Meaning in Tragedy." *Smithsonian Magazine.* December 2018. https://www.smithsonianmag.com/innovation/march-for-our-lives-student-activists-showed-meaning-tragedy-180970717/.

Knell, Yolanda. "Egypt's revolution: 18 days in Tahrir Square." *BBC News*. January 25, 2012. https://www.bbc.com/news/world-middle-east-16716089.

Lewis, Jerry M. and Thomas R. Hensley. "The May 4 Shootings at Kent State University: The Search for Historical Accuracy." *Kent State University*. Accessed on June 8, 2020. https://www.kent.edu/may-4-historical-accuracy.

PBS. WGBH Educational Foundation. "Timeline: What Led to the Tiananmen Square Massacre." *FRONTLINE Newsletter*. Accessed on June 10, 2020. https://www.pbs.org/wgbh/frontline/article/timeline-tiananmen-square/.

Riggs, William W. "Students for a Democratic Society." *The First Amendment Encyclopedia – Middle Tennessee State University*. Accessed June 8, 2020. https://www.mtsu.edu/first-amendment/article/1201/students-for-a-democratic-society.

Shabad, Rebecca, Chelsea Bailey, and Phil McCausland. "At March for Our Lives, Survivors Lead Hundreds of Thousands in Call for Change." *NBC News*. March 24, 2018. https://www.nbcnews.com/news/us-news/march-our-lives-draws-hundreds-thousands-washington-around-nation-n859716.

The Stanford Encyclopedia of Philosophy, Winter 2019 ed., s.v. "Max Weber," by Kim, Sung Ho. Edited by Zalta, Edward N. Accessed June 8, 2020. https://plato.stanford.edu/archives/win2019/entries/weber/.

"Tiananmen Square: What Happened in the Protests of 1989?" *BBC News.* June 4, 2019. https://www.bbc.com/news/world-asia-48445934.

"Tiananmen Square Protests." *A&E Television Networks.* Accessed on June 8, 2020, https://www.history.com/topics/china/tiananmen-square.

University of Michigan. "The Military Draft During the Vietnam War." *Michigan in the World.* Accessed June 8, 2020. http://michiganintheworld.history.lsa.umich.edu/antivietnamwar/exhibits/show/exhibit/draft_protests/the-military-draft-during-the-.

"Vietnam War Protests." *A&E Television Networks.* Accessed on June 8, 2020. https://www.history.com/topics/vietnam-war/vietnam-war-protests.

CHAPTER 3

Afrika Youth Movement. "About Us." Accessed June 8, 2020. https://afrikayouthmovement.org/about-us/.

Anderson, Janna and Lee Rainie. "The Positives of Digital Life." Pew Research Center. July 3, 2018. https://www.pewresearch.org/internet/2018/07/03/the-positives-of-digital-life/.

BBC. "China Uighurs: Detainees 'Free' after 'Graduating,' Official Says." December 9, 2019. https://www.bbc.com/news/world-asia-china-50712126.

BBC. "Data Leak Reveals How China 'Brainwashes' Uighurs in Prison Camps." November 24, 2019. https://www.bbc.com/news/world-asia-china-50511063.

Gallagher, Erin. "#MarchForOurLives & #NeverAgain." Medium. March 25, 2018. https://medium.com/@erin_gallagher/marchforourlives-neveragain-a59ee4a078cb.

Gettleman, Jeffrey, Sameer Yasir, Suhasini Raj, and Hari Kumar. "How Delhi's Police Turned Against Muslims." The New York Times. March 12, 2020. https://www.nytimes.com/2020/03/12/world/asia/india-police-muslims.html.

International Telecommunications Union. "Statistics." United Nations. Accessed June 8, 2020. https://www.itu.int/en/ITU-D/Statistics/Pages/stat/default.aspx.

Ives, Mike and Alexandra Stevenson. "Hong Kong Police Face Criticism Over Force Used at Protests." The New York Times. June 13, 2019. https://www.nytimes.com/2019/06/13/world/asia/hong-kong-extradition.html.

Kuchay, Bilal. "What You Should Know about India's 'Anti-Muslim' Citizenship Law." Al Jazeera. December 16, 2019. https://www.aljazeera.com/news/2019/12/india-anti-muslim-citizenship-bill-191209095557419.html.

Levitin, Michael. "The Triumph of Occupy Wall Street." The Atlantic. June 10, 2015. https://www.theatlantic.com/politics/archive/2015/06/the-triumph-of-occupy-wall-street/395408/.

Library of Congress. "Tactics and Techniques of the National Woman's Party Suffrage Campaign." Accessed June 8, 2020. https://www.loc.gov/static/collections/women-of-protest/images/tactics.pdf.

Mayault, Isabelle. "How a Pan-African Network of Cyber Activists Has Been Strengthening Democracy Online." Quartz Africa. June 2, 2018. https://qz.com/africa/1216713/pan-african-activists-network-africtivists-fight-online-to-strengthen-democracy-in-africa/.

Mirza, M. Usman, Andries Richter, Egbert H. van Nes, and Marten Scheffer. "Technology-driven inequality leads to poverty and resource depletion." *Ecological Economics* 160, no. 1 (June 2016): 215-226. https://doi.org/10.1016/j.ecolecon.2019.02.015

Sommeiller, Estelle and Mark Price. "The New Gilded Age: Income Inequality in the U.S. by State, Metropolitan Area, and County." Economic Policy Institute. July 19, 2018. https://www.epi.org/publication/the-new-gilded-age-income-inequality-in-the-u-s-by-state-metropolitan-area-and-county/.

Stanford University. "The Digital Divide." Accessed June 8, 2020. https://cs.stanford.edu/people/eroberts/cs181/projects/digital-divide/start.html.

Tufekci, Zeynep. "Online Social Change: Easy to Organize, Hard to Win." Filmed October 2014 in Rio de Janeiro, Brazil. TED Video. https://www.ted.com/talks/zeynep_tufekci_online_social_change_easy_to_organize_hard_to_win.

Vandyck, Charles and Ngnaoussi Elongue Cédric Christian. "Social Movement and Social Change in Africa." *WACSERIES*

Op-Ed. West African Civil Society Institute. April 3, 2019. https://
www.researchgate.net/publication/333673775_Social_Movement_
and_Social_Change_in_Africa.

CHAPTER 4

Adichie, Chimamanda Ngozi. *We Should All Be Feminists.* New
York: Vintage Books by Random House LLC, 2014.32.

Ay, Pinar, Osman Hayran, Ahmet Topuzoglu, Seyhan Hidiroglu,
Anahit Coskun, Dilsad Save, Hacer Nalbant, Erhan Ozdemir, and
Levent Eker. "The influence of Gender Roles On Health-Seeking
Behaviour during Pregnancy in Turkey." *The European Journal
of Contraception and Reproductive Health Care* 14, no. 4 (August
2009): 290-300. https://doi.org/10.1080/13625180902925211.

Barry, Aoife. "'I Tell People: Girls and Women in Patriarchal
Societies, They Die as if They Were Never Born.'" *The* Journal.ie,
November 19, 2018. https://www.thejournal.ie/interview-ziauddin-
yousafzai-4343172-Nov2018/.

Baumgarten, Maryann. "The Key Role of Sponsorship." SLAC
National Accelerator Laboratory, Stanford University, accessed
June 8, 2020. https://inclusion.slac.stanford.edu/sites/inclusion.
slac.stanford.edu/files/The_Key_Role_of_a_Sponsorship_for_
Diverse_Talent.pdf.

Bishop-Josef, Sandra, Chris Beakey, Sara Watson, and Tom
Garrett. "Want to Grow the Economy? Fix the Child Care Crisis." Ready Nation, Council for a Strong America, January 2019.
https://strongnation.s3.amazonaws.com/documents/602/83bb2275-
ce07-4d74-bcee-ff6178daf6bd.pdf?1547054862&inline;%20file-

name=%22Want%20to%20Grow%20the%20Economy?%20Fix%20
the%20Child%20Care%20Crisis.pdf%22.

Carroll, Joseph. "Americans Satisfied with Number of Friends,
Closeness of Friendships." *Gallup.* March 5, 2004. https://news.
gallup.com/poll/10891/americans-satisfied-number-friends-close-
ness-friendships.aspx.

Department for International Development. "REACH: Challenging Barriers to Health Care." January 1, 2005. https://www.gov.
uk/dfid-research-outputs/reach-challenging-barriers-to-health-
care-in-malawi.

Foxx, Deja. "GenZ Girl Gang." Instagram. https://www.instagram.
com/genzgirlgang/?hl=en.

George, Linda K. "The Health-Promoting Effects of Social Bonds."
Duke University, 2016. https://www.cossa.org/caht-bssr/linda%20
george.pdf.

Girls Empowerment Network. "The Importance of Mentors for
Girls and Young Women." February 4, 2015. https://www.girlse-
mpowermentnetwork.org/blog/the-importance-of-mentors-for-
girls-and-young-women.

Girls Not Brides. "Celebrating Change-makers: Angeline, Putting
Girls at the Centre of Change in Zimbabwe." June 7, 2017. https://
www.girlsnotbrides.org/change-makers-angeline-makore-zim-
babwe/.

Greif, Geoffrey and Tanya L. Sharpe. "The Friendships of Women:
Are There Differences between African Americans and Whites?"

Journal of Human Behavior in the Social Environment 20, no. 6, (2010):791–807. doi: 10.1080/10911351003751892.

Halpin, John, Karl Agne, and Margie Omero. "Affordable Child Care and Early Learning for All Families." Center for American Progress. 2018. https://cdn.americanprogress.org/content/uploads/2018/09/12074422/ChildCarePolling-report.pdf.

Hill, Lilian H. and Celeste A. Wheat. "The Influence of Mentorship and Role Models on University Women Leaders' Career Paths to University Presidency." *The Qualitative Report* 22, no. 8 (2008): 2090-2111. https://login.proxy.lib.duke.edu/login?url=https://search.proquest.com/docview/1929693822?accountid=10598.

IbnSina and ICRH. "KAP Survey Regarding Reproductive Health." October 2002. Accessed June 8, 2020. http://icrhm.org/sites/default/files/KAPsurveyKabulICRHIbnSina.pdf.

Kumi-Kyereme, Akwasi, Kofi Awusabo-Asare, Ann Biddlecom, and Augustine Tanle. "Influence of Social Connectedness, Communication and Monitoring on Adolescent Sexual Activity in Ghana." *African Journal of Reproductive Health* 11, no. 1 (April 2007): 133-136. https://www.ncbi.nlm.nih.gov/pmc/articles/PMC2367144/.

Kyilleh, Joseph Maaminu, Philip Teg-Nefaah Tabong, and Benson Boinkum Konlaan. "Adolescents' Reproductive Health Knowledge, Choices and Factors Affecting Reproductive Health Choices: a Qualitative Study in the West Gonja District in Northern Region, Ghana." *BMC International Health and Human Rights* 18, no. 6 (2018). https://doi.org/10.1186/s12914-018-0147-5.

Latifnejad Roudsari, Robab, Mojgan Javadnoori, Marzieh Hasanpour, Seyyed Mohammad Mehdi Hazavehei, and Ali Taghipour. "Socio-cultural Challenges to Sexual Health Education for Female Adolescents in Iran." *Iranian Journal of Reproductive Medicine* 11, no. 2 (2013): 101-10. https://www.ncbi.nlm.nih.gov/pmc/articles/PMC3941358/.

Mohammed, Rehab. "What Is Barriers to Women Advancement?" Empower Women: Community Discussions. Last Modified December 24.2016. https://www.empowerwomen.org/en/community/discussions/2016/12/what-is-barriers-to-women-advancement.

Monserrat, Silvia, Jo Ann Duffy, Miguel Olivas-Luján, John Miller, Ann Gregory, Suzy Fox, Terri Lituchy, Betty Punnett, and Neusa Santos. "Mentoring Experiences of Successful Women across the Americas." *Gender in Management: An International Journal* 24, no. 6 (August 2009): 455-476. doi: 10.1108/17542410910980414.

Plan International Canada Inc. "Plan International: What We Do." Last modified 2019. https://plancanada.ca/what-we-do?_ga=2.159115450.1885136033.1581879015-2006363762.1581879015.

Raising Children: An Australian Parenting Website. "Friends and Friendship: 10 Frequently Asked Questions." Last modified November 17, 2017. https://raisingchildren.net.au/school-age/behaviour/friends-siblings/friends-faqs#3-my-child-has-only-a-few-close-friends-should-l-be-worried-nav-title.

Reczek, Corinne, Mieke Beth Thomeer, Amy C. Lodge, Debra Umberson, and Megan Underhill. "Diet and Exercise in Parenthood: A Social Control Perspective." *Journal of Marriage and the Family* 76, 5 (2014): 1047-1062. doi:10.1111/jomf.12135.

Sheikh, Shaheen and A. Furnham. "A Cross-Cultural Study of Mental Health Beliefs and Attitudes toward Seeking Professional Help." *Soc Psychiatry Psychiatric Epidemiology* 35, no. 1 (2000): 326-334. https://doi.org/10.1007/s001270050246.

Synovitz, Ron. "Afghanistan: Gender Taboos Keep Women from Seeking Medical Care." Radio Free Europe. March 3, 2004. Accessed June 8, 2020.

Thomas, Patricia A., Hiu Liu, and Debra Umberson. "Family Relationships and Well-Being." *Innovation in Aging* 1, no. 3 (November 2017), 1-11. doi:10.1093/geroni/igx025. https://www.ncbi.nlm.nih.gov/pmc/articles/PMC5954612/pdf/igx025.pdf.

UK Essays. "The Barriers for Women in Career Advancement." Last modified December 1, 2018. https://www.ukessays.com/essays/spanish/the-barriers-for-women-in-career-advancement.php#citethis.

United Nations, "Emma Watson at the HeForShe Campaign 2014— Official UN Video," September 22, 2014, video, 13:15. https://www.youtube.com/watch?v=gkjW9PZBRfk.

United Nations Funds for Public Activities. "Issue 7: Women Empowerment." (Cairo, UNFPA, 1994). https://www.unfpa.org/resources/issue-7-women-empowerment#.

United Nations. "HeforShe." UN Women. Accessed June 8, 2020. https://www.heforshe.org/en/movement.

United Nations Statistics Division. "Chapter 5: The Power and Decision-Making." *The World's Women 2015*, (2015). 119-138. https://

unstats.un.org/unsd/gender/downloads/WorldsWomen2015_chapter5_t.pdf.

Unite for Sight. "Module 1: Family Dynamics and Health." Unite for Sight. Last modified 2020. http://www.uniteforsight.org/gender-power/module1.

UN Women. "HeforShe Equality Story: Redefining Masculinity in Jordan." September 27, 2016. Video, 2:44. https://www.youtube.com/watch?v=-ePQiymLSNk&feature=youtu.be.

UN Women. "HeforShe Equality Story: Cycling for Gender Equality in Rural India." September 27, 2016. Video, 2:11. https://www.youtube.com/watch?time_continue=1&v=ken3B1FNkZo&feature=emb_logo.

Zimbabwe National Statistics Agency. "Zimbabwe Demographic and Health Survey 2015:Final Report" (Rockville, Maryland, U.S.A.: Zimbabwe National Statistics Agency (ZIMSTAT) and ICF International), November 2016. https://www.dhsprogram.com/pubs/pdf/FR322/FR322.pdf.

CHAPTER 5

Brown, Brené. *The Gifts of Imperfection: Let Go of Who You Think You're Supposed to Be and Embrace Who You Are.* Center City: Hazelden, 2010.

Corsaro, William A. *The Sociology of Childhood.* Los Angeles: SAGE Publications, 2010.

Foutty, Janet, Terri Cooper, and Shelley Zalis. "Redefining Leadership: The Inclusion Imperative," Deloitte, June 2018, accessed June 8, 2020. https://www2.deloitte.com/content/dam/Deloitte/us/Documents/about-deloitte/us-shift-forward-redefining-leadership.pdf.

Khattab, Jasmien. "Why It's Harder for Women to Be Seen as Authentic, Effective Leaders." Rotterdam School of Management, Erasmus University. June 27, 2017. https://discovery.rsm.nl/articles/287-why-its-harder-for-women-to-be-seen-as-authentic-effective-leaders/.

Myna Mahila Foundation, accessed June 8, 2020.https://mynamahila.com/.

The Women's Foundation. "Authenticity." June 12, 2018. https://twfhk.org/blog/authenticity.

Varga, Somogy and Charles Guignon. "Authenticity." *The Stanford Encyclopedia of Philosophy,* Edited by Edward N. Zalta. Spring 2020, accessed June 8, 2020. https://plato.stanford.edu/entries/authenticity/#OriMeaConAut.

CHAPTER 6

Black, Michele C., Kathleen C. Basile, Matthew J. Breiding, Sharon G. Smith Mikel L. Walters, Melissa T. Merrick Jieru Chen, and Mark R. Stevens. *The National Intimate Partner and Sexual Violence Survey (NISVS): 2010 Summary Report.* National Center for Injury Prevention and Control, Centers for Disease Control and Prevention. November 2011. https://www.cdc.gov/violenceprevention/pdf/NISVS_Report2010-a.pdf.

Foxx, Deja. Interview by Asha Dahya. "Exclusive Interview with Deja Foxx – Teen Activist, Change-Maker, & Future Political Leader." *GirlTalkHQ*, April 27, 2017. https://www.girltalkhq.com/exclusive-interview-deja-foxx-teen-activist-change-maker-future-political-leader/.

García-Moreno, Claudia, Christina Pallitto, Karen Devries, Heidi Stöckl, Charlotte Watts, and Naeemah Abrahams, "Global and Regional Estimates of Violence against Women: Prevalence and Health Effects of Intimate Partner Violence and Non-Partner Sexual Violence," Department of Reproductive Health and Research, World Health Organization, Edited by Penny Howes. 2013. https://www.who.int/reproductivehealth/publications/violence/9789241564625/en/.

Girls Not Brides. "Child Marriage Around the World." Accessed June 8, 2020. https://www.girlsnotbrides.org/where-does-it-happen/.

Institute for Policy Studies. "Economic Inequality Across Gender Diversity." Inequality.org. Accessed June 8, 2020. https://inequality.org/gender-inequality/.

Inter-Agency Task Force on Rural Women. "Facts & Figures: Rural Women and the Millennium Development Goals." UN Womenwatch. Accessed June 8, 2020. https://www.un.org/womenwatch/feature/ruralwomen/facts-figures.html.

Klein, Sarah. "This Instagram Activist Is Smashing the Stigma on Depression: 'I Want to Change the Narrative of a Picture-Perfect life.'" Health.com. May 29, 2018. https://www.health.com/condi-

tion/depression/real-life-strong-sad-girls-club-depression-elyse-
fox.

Women, Business, and the Law. *Workplace, 2020*. The World Bank.
Accessed June 8, 2020. .https://wbl.worldbank.org/en/data/explore-
topics/wbl_sj

CHAPTER 7

ACVEO. "About." Accessed June 8, 2020. https://www.acevo.org.
uk/about/.

Confino, Jo. "Report Shows Companies Still Don't Take Climate
Change Seriously." *The Guardian*. September 12, 2013. https://www.
theguardian.com/sustainable-business/blog/cdp-report-compa-
nies-emissions-failing.

Department of Economic and Social Affairs. "Climate Change."
United Nations. Accessed June 8, 2020. https://www.un.org/devel-
opment/desa/indigenouspeoples/climate-change.html.

Duckworth, Angela, Christopher Peterson, Michael Matthews,
and Dennis Kelly, "Grit: Perseverance and Passion for Long-Term
Goals." *Journal of Personality and Social Psychology* 92, no.6 (2007):
1087-1101. 10.1037/0022-3514.92.6.1087.

Eurich, Tasha. *Insight: The Surprising Truth About How Others
See Us, How We See Ourselves, and Why the Answers Matter More
Than We Think*. (New York: Crown, 2017).

Eurich, Tasha. Interviewed by Chad Gordon. "The Importance of
Self-Awareness with Tasha Eurich." *Blanchard LeaderChat*, Feb-

ruary 1, 2019. https://leaderchat.org/2019/02/01/the-importance-of-self-awareness-with-tasha-eurich/.

Gates, Bill. "Teachers Need Real Feedback." Filmed May 2013 in New York, NY. TED Video. 00:31. https://www.ted.com/talks/bill_gates_teachers_need_real_feedback?language=en.

Glangchai, Cristal. "The Importance of Showing Girls It's OK to Fail." *Quartz*. April 26, 2018. https://qz.com/work/1261847/teaching-girls-that-its-ok-to-fail-is-important-for-their-success/.

Institute for Children, Poverty, & Homelessness. "On the Map: The Atlas of Student Homelessness in New York City 2017." August 14, 2017. https://www.icphusa.org/reports/map-atlas-student-homelessness-new-york-city-2017/.

Kauflin, Jeff. "Only 15% of People Are Self-Aware—Here's How to Change." *Forbes*. May 10, 2017. https://www.forbes.com/sites/jeffkauflin/2017/05/10/only-15-of-people-are-self-aware-heres-how-to-change/#7c95a1862b8c.

McGill, Bryant. *Simple Reminders: Inspiration for Living Your Best Life*. SRN, 2015.

Me Too Movement. "History and Vision." Accessed June 8, 2020. https://metoomvmt.org/about/.

Merriman, Kimberly. *Leadership and Perseverance*. 2017. 10.1007/978-3-319-31036-7_19.335. https://www.researchgate.net/publication/318034785_Leadership_and_Perseverance.

National Center for Women and Information Technology. "Institutional Barriers & Their Effects: How Can I Talk to Colleagues about These Issues?" May 6, 2009. https://www.ncwit.org/resources/institutional-barriers-their-effects-how-can-i-talk-colleagues-about-these-issues.

Penney, Joe. "The Fight for Justice Takes Its Toll on Ferguson Activists." *New York Review Daily.* February 12, 2019. Https://Www.Nybooks.Com/Daily/2019/02/12/The-Fight-For-Justice-Takes-Its-Toll-On-Ferguson-Activists/.

Sobieszczuk, Dorota. Interviewed by Corey Harnish. "How to find your inner Change-Maker: Story of Dorota." *Better World International,* July 11, 2017. https://www.betterworldinternational.org/blog/interview-changemaker-dorota/.

Sun, Xavier. "Taiwan Soon to be Plastic Free." *Waste Not Asia* no. 1 (2018): 16-20.

The Re-Earth Initiative. "Meet the Team." Accessed June 8, 2020. https://reearthin.org/team.

Tibballs, Sue. "12 Habits of Successful Change-Makers: Persistence, Perseverance & Resilience." ACVEO. April 18, 2019.https://www.acevo.org.uk/2019/04/12-habits-of-successful-change-makers-persistence-perseverance-resilience/.

VentureGirls. "Meet Dr. Glangchai." Accessed June 8, 2020. http://www.venturegirls.org/books/dr-cristal.

Williamson, Marianne. *A Return to Love: Reflections on the Principles of "A Course in Miracles."* New York: Harper Collins, 2009.

Yeung, Jessie, Erin Chan, and Michelle Lim. "Young People across Asia Pushed for Change in 2019. Meet Five of Them." CNN. December 26, 2019. https://edition.cnn.com/2019/12/25/asia/asia-youth-activists-2019-intl-hnk-scli/index.html.

CHAPTER 8

A Mighty Girl. "About." Accessed June 8, 2020. https://www.amightygirl.com/about.

Adichie, Chimamanda. "The Danger of a Single Story." Filmed July 2009 in Oxford, UK. TED Video. 00:32.;1:36;10:04. https://www.ted.com/talks/chimamanda_ngozi_adichie_the_danger_of_a_single_story?language=en.

Antony, Valsamma. "Education and employment: The key to Women's Empowerment." *Kurukshetra, Journal of Ministry of Rural Development*. 2006.

Chow, Kat. "'Model Minority' Myth Again Used as a Racial Wedge Between Asians And Blacks." *NPR*. April 19, 2017. https://www.npr.org/sections/codeswitch/2017/04/19/524571669/model-minority-myth-again-used-as-a-racial-wedge-between-asians-and-blacks.

Combaz, Emilie and Claire Mcloughlin. "Social and Economic Empowerment." GSDRC. August 2014. https://gsdrc.org/topic-guides/voice-empowerment-and-accountability/supplements/social-and-economic-empowerment/.

Girls Empowerment Network. "About Us." Accessed June 8, 2020. https://www.girlsempowermentnetwork.org/about-us/mission.

Kim, Claire Jean. Interviewed by Kat Chow. "Model Minority' Myth Again Used as a Racial Wedge Between Asians And Blacks." *NPR*. April 19, 2017. https://www.npr.org/sections/codeswitch/2017/04/19/524571669/model-minority-myth-again-used-as-a-racial-wedge-between-asians-and-blacks.

Kossler, Karla, Lindsay M. Kuroki, Jenifer E. Allsworth, Gina M. Secura, Kimberly A. Roehl, and Jeffrey F. Peipert. "Perceived Racial, Socioeconomic and Gender Discrimination and Its Impact on Contraceptive Choice," *Contraception* 84, no. 3 (2011): 273-9. doi: 10.1016/j.contraception.2011.01.004.

Mandal, Keshab Chandra. "Concept and Types of Women Empowerment." *International Forum of Teaching and Studies* 9, no. 2 (2013). http://americanscholarspress.us/journals/IFST/pdf/IFOTS-2-2013/IFOTS_v9_n2_art3.pdf.

Merriam-Webster. s.v. "tokenism (n.)." Accessed June 8, 2020. https://www.merriam-webster.com/dictionary/tokenism.

Office of Disease Prevention and Health Promotion. "Discrimination." Accessed June 8, 2020. https://www.healthypeople.gov/2020/topics-objectives/topic/social-determinants-health/interventions-resources/discrimination.

Srivastava, R.S. "Women Empowerment: Some Critical Issue." Edited by Abha Avasti and A.K. Srivastava. *Modernity, Feminism, and Women Empowerment.* Rawat Publications. 2001.

Women for Women International. "Our Approach." Accessed June 8, 2020. https://www.womenforwomen.org/our-approach.

Women for Women International. "Social Empowerment."
Accessed June 8, 2020. https://www.womenforwomen.org/what-
we-do/programs/social-empowerment.

CHAPTER 9

Abrams, Lindsay. "Study: Praise Children for What They Do, Not
Who They Are." *The Atlantic*. February 12, 2013. https://www.the-
atlantic.com/health/archive/2013/02/study-praise-children-for-
what-they-do-not-who-they-are/273062/.

Ashley, Erika. "Female Disruptors: The Colored Girl Is Empowering Women of Color to Thrive." *Authority Magazine*. Medium.
October 9, 2018. https://medium.com/authority-magazine/female-
disruptors-the-colored-girl-is-bridging-the-gap-between-people-
of-color-and-their-audiences-4269f15609d6.

Halvorson, Heidi Grant. "The Trouble with Bright Girls." *Psychology Today*. January 27, 2011. https://www.psychologytoday.com/us/
blog/the-science-success/201101/the-trouble-bright-girls.

Mishra, Gunjan. "The Psychological Facets of Women Empowerment at Workplace." *International Journal of Recent Trends in
Engineering & Research 2*, no. 11 (2016).https://www.ijrter.com/
papers/volume-2/issue-11/the-psychological-facets-of-women-em-
powerment-at-workplace.pdf.

Moonie, Neil. *GCE AS Level Health and Social Care Single Award
Book (For OCR)*. Oxford: Heinemann, 2005. 5.

Mruk, Christopher J. *Self-Esteem and Positive Psychology, 4th Edition*. New York: Springer, 2013. 188.

Musa, Zara Mallam, Aminah Ahmad, Siti Zobidah Omar, and Abubakar Musa. "Psychological Empowerment and Engagement in Income-Generating Activities among Rural Women in Yobe State, Nigeria." *IOSR Journal of Humanities and Social Science* 22, no.10 (2016):70-84. https://pdfs.semanticscholar.org/2849/fb1514005d8929aca6a240c6adda1041986a.pdf.

CHAPTER 10

Abuya, Benta A., James Ciera, and Elizabeth Kimani-Murage. "Effect of Mother's Education on Child's Nutritional Status in the Slums of Nairobi." *BMC Pediatrics* 12, no. 80 (2012). https://doi.org/10.1186/1471-2431-12-80.

"Birth Control," *Sex, Explained,* Netflix, Vox, January 2, 2020. https://www.netflix.com/title/81160763.

Busby, Eleanor. "Students Are Turning to Sex Work for Extra Money but Experts Warn Universities Are Ignoring the Issue." *Independent.* December 26, 2018. https://www.independent.co.uk/news/education/education-news/students-sex-work-prostitution-webcam-university-tuition-fees-education-a8614186.html.

Chiyaka, Tarisai, Phillis Mushati, Bernadette Hensen, Sungai Chabata, James R. Hargreaves, Sian Floyd, Isolde J. Birdthistle, et al. "Reaching Young Women Who Sell Sex: Methods and Results of Social Mapping to Describe and Identify Young Women for DREAMS Impact Evaluation in Zimbabwe." PLOS ONE. March 15, 2018. https://doi.org/10.1371/journal.pone.0194301.

Khattak, Umme K., Saima P. Iqbal, and Haider Ghazanfar. "The Role of Parents' Literacy in Malnutrition of Children Under the

Age of Five Years in a Semi-Urban Community of Pakistan: A Case-Control Study." *Cureus* 9, no. 6 (2017). doi:10.7759/cureus.1316.

Kirya, Julius. "Women's Empowerment: The Key to Social and Economic Development." Global Health Corps. March 31, 2015. https:// ghcorps.org/women-empowerment-the-key-to-social-and-economic-development/.

Lailulo, Yishak Abraham, A. Sathiya Susuman, and Renette Blignaut. "Correlates of Gender Characteristics, Health and Empowerment of Women in Ethiopia." *BMC Women's Health* 15, no.116 (2015). https://doi.org/10.1186/s12905-015-0273-3.

Mushi, Ruth. "Student Money Survey 2018—Results." Save the Student. Updated October 16, 2018. https://www.savethestudent. org/money/student-money-survey-2018.html.

OECD. "Gender Equality in Education, Employment and Entrepreneurship: Final Report to the MCM 2012," 2012. http://www. oecd.org/employment/50423364.pdf.

Rao, P.H. Sethumadhava. "Education for Women's Empowerment." Edited by Promilla Kapur. *Empowering the Indian Women*. Ministry of Information and Broadcasting, Government of India, New Delhi. 2001.

Semahegn, Agumasie, Kwasi Torpey, Abubakar Manu, Nega Assefa, Gezahegn Tesfaye, and Augustine Ankomah. "Are Interventions Focused on Gender-Norms Effective in Preventing Domestic Violence against Women in Low and Lower-Middle Income countries? A Systematic Review and Meta-Analysis." *Reproductive Health* 16, no. 93 (2019). https://doi.org/10.1186/s12978-019-0726-5.

Simbar, Masoumeh, Shiva Alizadeh, Mahboubeh Hajifoghaha, and Fatemeh Dabiri. "Comparison of Social, Economic and Familial Empowerment in Married Women in Three Cities of Iran." *International Journal of Community-Based Nursing and Midwifery* 5, no. 3 (2017): 248-255. https://www.ncbi.nlm.nih.gov/pmc/articles/PMC5478745/.

The World Bank. "Not Educating Girls Costs Countries Trillions of Dollars, Says New World Bank Report." July 11, 2018. https://www.worldbank.org/en/news/press-release/2018/07/11/not-educating-girls-costs-countries-trillions-of-dollars-says-new-world-bank-report.

UNESCO. "2010 Education for All Global Monitoring Report—Reaching the Marginalized." Accessed June 8, 2020. .https://unesdoc.unesco.org/ark:/48223/pf0000187279.

UNESCO. "Global Education Monitoring Report." Accessed June 8, 2020. https://gem-report-2017.unesco.org/en/chapter/gender_monitoring_participation-and-completion/.

World Health Organization. "Maternal Mortality." September 19, 2019. https://www.who.int/news-room/fact-sheets/detail/maternal-mortality.

CHAPTER 11

AAUW. "An Underreported Problem: Campus Sexual Misconduct." Accessed June 9, 2020. https://www.aauw.org/resources/article/underreported-sexual-misconduct/.

Black, Michele C., Kathleen C. Basile, Matthew J. Breiding, Sharon G. Smith Mikel L. Walters, Melissa T. Merrick Jieru Chen, and Mark R. Stevens. *The National Intimate Partner and Sexual Violence Survey (NISVS): 2010 Summary Report.* National Center for Injury Prevention and Control, Centers for Disease Control and Prevention. November 2011. https://www.cdc.gov/violenceprevention/pdf/NISVS_Report2010-a.pdf.

CARE. "Mission and Vision." Accessed June 9, 2020. https://www.care.org/about/mission-vision.

de la O Campos, Ana Paula and Nynne Warring. "Gender and Land Statistics: Recent developments in FAO's Gender and Land Rights Database." FAO. United Nations. 2015. http://www.fao.org/3/a-i4862e.pdf.

FAO, Gender and Land Statistics Recent Developments in FAO's Gender and Land Rights Database (Rome, 2015). http://www.fao.org/3/a-i4862e.pdf.

Feldman, Sarah. "Steady Rise for Women in STEM but Gender Gap Remains." Statista. February 11, 2019. https://www.statista.com/chart/16970/women-stem/.

Gluckman, Nell. "Students Say They Don't Trust Campus Title IX Processes. And They Doubt Their Own Reports Would Be Taken Seriously." *The Chronicle of Higher Education.* October 23, 2019. https://www.chronicle.com/article/Students-Say-They-Don-t/247399.

Khazan, Olga. "The More Gender Equality, the Fewer Women in STEM." *The Atlantic.* February 18, 2018. https://www.theatlantic.

com/science/archive/2018/02/the-more-gender-equality-the-fewer-women-in-stem/553592/.

Krentz, Matt, Olivier Wierzba, Katie Abouzahr, Jennifer Garcia-Alonso, and Frances Taplett. "Five Ways Men Can Improve Gender Diversity at Work." Boston Consulting Group. October 10, 2017. https://www.bcg.com/en-us/publications/2017/people-organization-behavior-culture-five-ways-men-improve-gender-diversity-work.aspx.

Mandal, Keshab Chandra. "Concept and Types of Women Empowerment." International Forum of Teaching and Studies 9, no. 2 (2013). http://americanscholarspress.us/journals/IFST/pdf/IFOTS-2-2013/IFOTS_v9_n2_art3.pdf

Messing, Karen. "Do Men and Women Have Different Jobs Because of Their Biological Differences?" International Journal of Health Services 12, no.1 (1982). https://doi.org/10.2190%2FKK50-HCTC-9YHA-BUTA.

National Girls Collaborative Project. "The State of Girls and Women in STEM." March 2018. https://ngcproject.org/sites/default/files/ngcp_the_state_of_girls_and_women_in_stem_2018a.pdf.

RAINN. "Campus Sexual Violence: Statistics." Accessed June 9, 2020. https://www.rainn.org/statistics/campus-sexual-violence.

Sánchez- Páramo, Carolina and Ana Maria Munoz-Boudet. "No, 70% of the World's Poor Aren't Women, but That Doesn't Mean Poverty Isn't Sexist." World Bank Blogs. March 8, 2018. https://blogs.worldbank.org/developmenttalk/no-70-world-s-poor-aren-t-women-doesn-t-mean-poverty-isn-t-sexist.

Self Employed Women's Association (SEWA). "About Us." Accessed June 9, 2020. http://www.sewa.org/About_Us.asp.

Stoet, Gijsbert and David C. Geary. "The Gender-Equality Paradox in Science, Technology, Engineering, and Mathematics Education." *Psychological Science* 29, no. 4 (2018). https://doi.org/10.1177%2F0956797617741719.

Taylor, Georgia and Paola Pereznieto. "Review of Evaluation Approaches and Methods Used by Interventions on Women and Girls' Economic Empowerment." Overseas Development Institute. March 2014. https://www.odi.org/sites/odi.org.uk/files/odi-assets/publications-opinion-files/8843.pdf.

Women, Business, and the Law. *Workplace, 2020.* The World Bank. Accessed June 8, 2020. https://wbl.worldbank.org/en/data/explore-topics/wbl_sj.

UN Women. "Facts and Figures: Economic Empowerment." Accessed June 9, 2020. https://www.unwomen.org/en/what-we-do/economic-empowerment/facts-and-figures.

UNESCO Institute for Statistics. "Women in Science." UNESCO. Accessed June 9, 2020. http://uis.unesco.org/en/topic/women-science.

Yonis, Nuriya. Interviewed by CARE. "Fighting Poverty & Drought with Honeybees." Uploaded November 11, 2011, YouTube Video. https://www.youtube.com/watch?v=cSR4IFSCcI8&list=PL_1TzcAmZQmioRAEUjiL6Q1J_beth2feZ&index=5.

CHAPTER 12

DeSilver, Drew. "U.S. trails most developed countries in voter turn-out." *Fact Tank,* Pew Research Center. May 21, 2018. https://www.pewresearch.org/fact-tank/2018/05/21/u-s-voter-turnout-trails-most-developed-countries/.

Dictionary.com. "Womxn." Accessed June 10, 2020. https://www.dictionary.com/browse/womxn.

Mandal, Keshab Chandra. "Concept and Types of Women Empowerment." *International Forum of Teaching and Studies* 9, no. 2 (2013). http://americanscholarspress.us/journals/IFST/pdf/IFOTS-2-2013/ IFOTS_v9_n2_art3.pdf.

Rutgers Eagleton Institute of Politics. "Women in the U.S. Congress 2020." Accessed June 10, 2020. https://cawp.rutgers.edu/women-us-congress-2020.

United Nations. "The Sustainable Development Goals Report 2019." United Nations. New York. 2019. https://doi.org/10.18356/55eb9109-en.

U.S. Census Bureau. "Quick Facts: United States – Age and Sex." Accessed June 10, 2020. https://www.census.gov/quickfacts/fact/table/US/LFE046218.

FINAL WORDS

Gates, Melinda. *The Moment of Lift: How Empowering Women Changes the World.* New York: Flatiron Books, 2019. p.27.

Mahadevan, Purvaja. "Empowering Women Rebuilding the Society." Civil Service India. Accessed June 10, 2020. https://www.civilserviceindia.com/subject/Essay/empowering-women-rebuilding-the-society.html.

Shiva, Mira. "Health Care in Last 50 Years and Women's Empowerment." Edited by Promilla Kapur. *Empowering the Indian Women.* Publications Division, Ministry of Information and Broadcasting, Government of India, New Delhi. 2001.

United Nations Development Programme. "Sustaining Human Progress: Reducing Vulnerabilities and Building Resilience." Human Development Report, 2014. http://hdr.undp.org/sites/default/files/hdr14-report-en-1.pdf.

World Health Organization. "Jakarta Declaration on Leading Health Promotion into the 21st Century." Accessed June 10, 2020. https://www.who.int/healthpromotion/conferences/previous/jakarta/declaration/en/.

Made in the USA
Monee, IL
18 August 2020

37872034R00149